Voices from the Past

Peter Mladinic

Better Than Starbucks
Publications

Voices from the Past

Copyright © 2023 by Peter Mladinic

All rights reserved. This book or any portion thereof may not be reproduced or used in any manner whatsoever without the express written permission of author and the publisher except for the use of brief quotations in a book review or scholarly journal.

First Printing: ISBN 978-1-7376219-6-6

Cover Image: Portrait of a Woman (1910) Egon Schiele

Better Than Starbucks Publications
3094 Adkins Forest Lane, Tallahassee, Florida 32322

For Elizabeth Frank

Table of Contents

The Veil Cycle	1
Heart's Desire	2
Unsolved Mystery	3
Rain	4
Chemical Spill	5
If	6
Flashlight	7
Young Executive	8
Evelyn	10
Blue Jacket	12
The Paragons Meet The Jesters	13
Leather	14
Love and Marriage	16
Older: Portland, Maine, 1971	18
My Life Is Not Perfect	20
Wake	22
Light Smoker	23
Scars	24
The Long Road from Is to Was	26
Poolside 1968	28
To Know, Know, Know Him	29
In Church	30
Lady	32
Reciprocity	33
The Dating Game	34
Schaeffer Wonders	36
Topsy	38
Autobiography	39
Sweet Seasons	40
Humpback	42
St. Francis	44
The Great Billy Williams	46
The Weather	48
Mai	49
Schaeffer and Sheila	52

The Pearls	54
Sext	56
Voices from the Past	57
Toddle	58
Extra Duty	60
Black Menace	62
The Glorious Present	64
Aroostook	65
The Invisible Man Plants a Kiss on the Forehead of Absence	66
George and the Dobermans	67
Sunbeams	68
Abandoned Tenements	69
Eleven Roses	70
Philip	71
Tennis Court 1958	72
Visitations from the Other Side	73
Lenny Bruce	76
Kids Change Everything	77
Table Talk	78
Sideview Mirror	79
White Oval	80
The Unholy Three	81
Raymond	82
Delicacy	83
Phone Numbers	84
Summer Night at Heron Lake	85
Two Neighbors	86
Albert Place	87
Soldier	88
The Door	90
Hillside Stranglers	91
Eighteen	92
Silent Film Actor	94
Oh Rosemarie	95
Obscene	96

His Agenda	97
Ozu	98
Speed Reader	99
A Man like a Tree	100
Leave	101
Sleeping with a Student	102
Capitalists	106
Richard Pryor	107
Negative	108
Sweating in the Freezer	110
Double Elegy	112
Third Wheel	113
Then I Remembered	114
Small Daughter	115
Revise	116
Ink Factory	117
James and Miss Q	118

Acknowledgements

About the Author

The Veil Cycle

Lori, we have dogs in common, music,
The Catholic Church.
In the church I went to, behind the altar,
long, jagged, messy white stains
on the big gray wall wore their vertical thrust
right around the big wood crucifix.
St. Mary's wasn't poor. You'd think
they could have got rid of that mess.
It didn't look like Christ on the cross
coming out of clouds. Years later,
one cloudy Sunday, when I went to the Walker
Art Center, all white walls,
big glass windows and light inside
for the Morris Louis veil cycle,
colors in fresh combinations,
lavender blue green orange black brown red
yellow gold, silky, buoyant, sensuous,
so unlike the church's gray wall's stains.
Louis lived in the Baltimore area.
I saw his work in Minneapolis.
You in Los Angeles love your dogs
and your music. On the Llano Estacado
I read your emails. We haven't talked
about the Church. I wanted to tell
you about the Morris Louis veil cycle.

Heart's Desire

I marvel how such a beautiful song
came from such an ugly place.
I'm thinking of the Avalons who sang
and recorded this iconic R&B ballad
some call Doo-wop, and Newport News
where the Avalons came from.
I stayed there briefly. It was rows of
dark wood rooming houses, movie
houses with triple X marquees, a police
station. Late one Saturday night, on
shore patrol, I saw a drunk white
guy tear up his fingerprints,
his bloody face and head after white
cops clubbed him. My Newport News
clashes with this song. You've
likely heard "soul on fire" in some song.
When the Avalons sing it in "Heart's Desire"
I feel it down to my toenails.

Unsolved Mystery

A kid lived in Baltimore, the early 1990s.
His mother fatally overdosed on heroin,
his father gave him to the kid's aunt,
who lost him. His name was Roland.
The aunt neglected him. You might say,
Let's see it. All I can say, she was absent.
It's hard to see him opening a fridge
and finding it empty, hard to say what
he did for food, or to see him waking up
on a mattress on the floor, or dressing,
or out with friends. He had no one.
He likely got strangled by a predator.
You'd like to think he's alive but likely
he died before age 12. He had nothing.
Have you ever looked in the eyes of
someone who has nothing? I haven't.
The predator's hands on Roland's throat
to keep him from telling, the fear in
Roland's eyes, then his blank eyes —
I only know he disappeared.

Rain

The Viking Bar had sawdust on the floor.
Martino's had waiters
with towels on their arms and the Mohawk
Tavern waiters' white jackets were cut
at the waist. Henry was at our table in
Martino's in Juarez, his Spanish passable.
Round, pale, he was with me
under a tarp in a grove of trees one
afternoon. The rain stopped.
We rode down dirt roads in Pinyon Draw,
which was green. It was tranquility
seeing, hearing the rain with Henry.

Chemical Spill

A belowdecks storeroom —
bottles and vials spilled from drawers
and shelves at sea in rough waters —
was locked three years.
Mr. May and Chief Payne said to go down
and clean it up. It was like a bunch of dead
little birds, the crinkled brown bags,
torn cardboard boxes, broken glass,
bulkheads and overhead peeling,
a sickly orange tinged with yellow,
tilted shelves we took apart
and got out, then started on the glass.
Our drill, like a jackhammer
in a laborer's grip tearing up concrete,
had clout. We stripped corroded rust,
sandblasted bulkheads, painted the deck.
I recall drilling away the bulkheads' rust.
Even masked, we must have inhaled toxic
particles. Years later a nurse who smoked
and drank said "Ninety-nine percent is our
DNA, heart, cancer . . . not damn thing
we can do about it."

If

If, upon returning to the mainland from the island,
you don't go and knock on their door
you'll always be
adrift between island and mainland shore,
always outside their door.

If you don't go where they are and knock
they'll go on with their lives.
Should some sight or sound remind them of you
it will be you don't care, you never loved them.

You tell yourself approaching that shore
I love, loved and will love them. They are better
left alone, going on as they have been
since the morning I set out from the mainland.
I had to. That much was clear.

If, upon returning to the mainland, you don't knock
on their door they'll go on, no thoughts of you,
except sight or sound remind them.
Their faces clear in memory. The ones you love.

Flashlight

On the big dark hanger deck of an LPH
more in it than on it, the dark
a mouth, the flashlight, you click it off.
There you are, all dark.
The deck goes, the passageways
the aft brow, the dock in cold daylight
Brooklyn goes, the Brooklyn Bridge,
tunnels wooded paths window sills
of the past. Dark is all,
you walk in that mouth
the light's beams all that come between
you and the dark. Your thumb moves
the tab down. No light, dark like you've
never been in, you click the tab, the light
on, you walk. The dark is everywhere.

Young Executive

This is about race, about me, a white man
writing about black men, older than I
when I was 18 in Cutler, Maine, in 1966.

This is about Marks, Harris, Guy, Brown
and Johnny Williams, youngest of these
men, sailors, as I was. I called Johnny Willie.

In his high-pitched voice he would say,
The kid's gonna be a young executive!
He wanted, after the navy, to work hard

and for that work be justly compensated,
what many, even most people want.
The kid's gonna be a young executive!

Most of the sailors on the base were white
as were most citizens in nearby Machias.
Racially, this area, 30 miles from Canada,

was overwhelmingly white. Of the sailors
I've mentioned Marks had the darkest skin.
He was married, as was Guy, a corpsman.

Both were married and had kids. Harris,
Willie and Brown and I lived in the barracks.
And another black sailor, Whitfield, lived

there, he may not have been there when
Willie was there. One night Willie drank
too much, and peed on the floor

between his bunk and his locker.
I mention it because it was an indication
of something wrong, of turmoil going on

in Willie, who worked with and for Brown,
as I did. Brown, a lifer, would say, when
civilians came to the warehouse,

not to give them anything extra. He
might have said, Don't give those civilians
shit, though he rarely swore. I think

a life in the navy was a refuge against
the racism outside for Roland Brown
and men like him. Though to me no one

was like him, and no one is like him.
It was so unsettling the afternoon Willie
came in drunk and got in Brown's face

eager to punch Brown. Willie, shorter, stockier
darker skinned in contrast to Brown's
lighter skin, could have beaten Brown up.

Brown said something to back Willie off.
It could have been big trouble. Brown
was tall, slightly stooped and wore a trim

mustache. He chewed gum and twirled
in one corner of his mouth a toothpick.
He often sang quietly to himself

in a high-pitched voice. We visited once
when stationed on ships in Norfolk.
It was good seeing Brown. I don't know

where Willie went after Cutler, I hear
the upbeat tone I heard back in '66.
The kid's gonna be a young executive!

Evelyn

Do you have a key word in your life?
Is it Evelyn, because your spouse is named
Evelyn? Is it love, is it God, or faith?

Until recently I never had a key word. Mine
is time. For someone else "be" is the word,
not a word, the word: to be or not to be,

not a question, the question. River, fire,
snow, limestone. Any word could be a key
word, it's all up to the person, the individual.

As I said, up till recently I didn't have one.
Mine's time. Someone else's might be life,
or eternity or silence. The library was big,

bright and silent, the Sunday morning I
walked out of the library, and on the bridge
met Evelyn. It was January and very cold.

In an enclosure she wrote her phone number
on a piece of paper. She wore a dark blue
parka with a fur-lined hood. Nineteen then

now seventy. We lived close to that bridge
then, now we don't. Now we live closer
to each other than a decade ago. Time,

last I saw her face to face a July afternoon
on a sidewalk above a freeway. Not at all
quiet, not terribly hot, not sweltering.

That morning on the bridge was freezing.
In the enclosure I got a good look at her
face and she handed me a piece of paper

with her number on it. She pulled back
the fur-lined hood, to reveal very dark
brown hair, strands in little wavy curls

above her forehead. She was walking
toward the library I'd just left. We met
on the bridge and ducked into the enclosure

a bright cold quiet Sunday morning, very
cold, freezing. Were there no enclosure
there may have been no phone number

on a piece of paper, no five year
rollercoaster romance, no Evelyn. Time's
my word, not love, not God. "Time

has come today," a winter Sunday morning
Evelyn. One could say the key word is life.

Blue Jacket

Abby Williams and Libby German, respectively ages 13 and 14, were close friends, and victims of a double homicide that occurred near Delphi, Indiana, in 2017.

Can you ever stop chattering about news,
weather and, what did you have for lunch?
and look at Libby and Abby. Their faces
in pictures resemble wanted posters. Their
bodies below the Monon bridge near Delphi.
Except what you'll see is the railroad ties
of the bridge, that one picture with Abby
on the bridge, then the one of evil incarnate
in a blue jacket, a hand in his jeans pocket.
You'll hear evil's voice; guys, down the hill.
You won't see Libby and Abby after evil took
their lives, you'll see the tilted winter trees
and leaf-strewn rocky ground. Mostly it's
the bridge, high, long, splintery, rickety
the girls walked, and evil followed, and led
them down the hill. You'll see no weapon,
you'll not know cause-of-death. The cops
know but are not releasing that, not yet.
Evil is white, young or middle-aged. A hood
under the jacket is up by his neck. He has
a full head of hair, a hand in one pocket.
You'll see and hear evil, see Abby in a pic
Libby took, who recorded evil's voice. Her
video hints evil had walked the Monon
High Bridge before. It's thought evil lives
in Delphi or nearby. You'll see steep hills,
trees that look like sticks and thicker trees,
all minus leaves. The ground strewn
with rocks and big brown leaves, mostly
you'll see the high, narrow, rickety bridge.
It looks scary to people afraid of heights.

The Paragons Meet The Jesters

Three kinds of people would steal my music:
the drug addict who sells it for drugs,
the music lover who sells it to a record shop
or adds it to their own collection,
and the person who wants it because
it's mine and they want to steal something
I love that's not part (or all) of my body
but part of my soul. The term
record shop signals vinyl, not a clunky 78
but a 45 disc such as I'd seen on a wall
at Swingin Slim's in a subway arcade off
Times Square. I bought the Swallows'
It Ain't the Meat It's the Motion, took it home
and up in my room with the door closed
danced to its jumpy rhythm, and to the
Dominoes' Tenderly with Jackie Wilson
on lead. Eyes closed I listened seeing Judy
Hyman's long face close to mine,
enraptured in her brunette beauty and
Jackie's strong smooth voice. The thief
took that from me because I'm me
alone in a room looking out windows
at green treetops and part of a gray river
that curves like an hourglass hip.
If they wanted even more they'd take an LP,
say, *The Paragons Meet The Jesters.*
They wouldn't sell it so they could stick
a needle in an arm in a gas station rest
room, but because it's mine, like that part
in R Kelly's Slow Dance "Let the record spin
round and round," a 45. Judy and I, she
taller by two inches, cling to its melodies
out on the floor in the school cafeteria.

Leather

When I was a kid, baseball all the rage,
I was lucky to have a few baseball gloves,
though one was a catcher's mitt. Round,
thick, never called a glove, it was different
from the standard infield / outfield glove
worn by Wille Mays, the Say Hey Kid,
when he caught the Vic Wertz long fly
to center — that catch an earthly miracle

to Polo Grounds fans. Distinct from Willie's
glove and the glove with which Yankees'
shortstop Tony Kubek scooped grounders,
the first base glove of Cleveland's Power,
first name Vic. That glove, banana-shaped,
folded, that fold needed to catch what was
hit, and mostly thrown, to first. It folds.
In form it was my favorite of the three types.

All three, different as they were and are,
have center pockets that have to be oiled.
Yesterday at the gym a tall brunette said
her husband had pitched for Texas Tech.
I didn't ask, did he oil his glove's pocket, but
you can bet he had to. All players do this.
Oil softens the leather, which makes a ball
easier to catch. I couldn't catch or pitch,

or hit. Still, I liked baseball. At one time
I had a glove with that banana shape, like
Vic Power's, also a catcher's mitt. Rawlings
and Spalding baseball gloves, I was lucky
to own more than one, lucky to live where
others, too, owned gloves. I never thought:
cows are killed so we can wear gloves.
I got a glove that looked like Whitey Ford's.

I squirted oil from a dropper into a pocket,
rubbed the oil in with my fingers. Gradually
a pocket darkened. It felt and looked good.
The dark shiny soft center where a ball
was caught. I don't own a glove now, but a
leather jacket is close by, only one. I don't
like that cows are slaughtered. Baseball
days, I was a kid, I didn't think of it at all.

Love and Marriage

Frank and Eileen's divorce was nasty,
as many are, but I wasn't in court,
hearing court. I imagined, had a film
in my mind, though I didn't see lawyers.
He wanted the divorce. Eileen had strayed
with one man, but likely more than one.
Men I never met. She told me last time
I visited, their marriage falling apart. Then
the divorce I heard about from her,
from him. I was two thousand miles away
from these two close friends. Gradually
he silently accused me, not saying outright
I wasn't there for him. What could I do,
holding down a job at times overwhelming
as jobs can be. I tried to be a good friend
but wasn't good enough. He retreated
into silence. But she and I stayed close
enough for me to know that they in time
fixed their problem. They didn't remarry
but resumed the friend part of marriage.
Both living in the town they lived in when
they lived on Castlewood, with their son
and daughter. Very recently the daughter
Lori reached out to me. Frank was living
in her house, with her family, and passed
after a long illness. I texted Eileen, told her
I connected with her daughter. That's cool
was all she texted back. When Frank
became ill she texted brief texts; like I
got a report of his decline, but that's all.

Once he was like a kid brother to me,
and she a sister. We met in Mr. Gilmore's
World History, which met at two, Monday
and Wednesday. They were a couple.
He had a red Volvo wagon, the Frank
Mobile, I sat in back while we rode long
straight country roads buzzed on the joints
we passed, some nights high on acid.
Flash forward, best man at their wedding
I raised a glass to a long happy marriage.
When Frank was ill, I thought about him
often, but what could I say, I'm sorry
you're dying. I didn't ask if I could talk
with him. There was the fact of his dying
nothing could change. I feel I've lost him
but what is a feeling compared to the fact
dead is dead. At least Lori reached out.
Their divorce she took hard being a kid
but I guess she got past it, as Frank
and Eileen got past it.

Older: Portland, Maine, 1971

Why did you have to look at him, lock eyes
walk your body near his, where exactly
in Portland were you when you showed him
your soul when your lips kissed his
that first time? Were you in a malt shop
or in a park's bandstand, with clouds
in the sky? Was it night or afternoon?

That Friday you came out of the music store
from visiting a friend who worked there,
what was it that made you open the door
of the blue Cadillac and get in back,
with him at the wheel, and another man,
Reid Parley riding shotgun. What was it?
You were sixteen and Everett, twenty two.

He'd have you home in time for supper.
What made you believe that lie, Cathy?
What kept you in the Caddy's back seat
looking out at trees, cars parked on streets
as you left that city? Why did you stay
when the Caddy slowed down, as it did,
why didn't you jump out and run away?

Why didn't you run when Reid, his hand
on the back of your neck, walked you
towards a gas station's restroom door?
Or when Everett got new tires on the car
he'd stolen, and paid with a credit card
also stolen, paid in a Fort Fairfield garage.
Why didn't you run? You were way up

in Aroostook, why didn't you loose your neck
from Reid's grip and run to a stranger
who could have called the law who in turn
could have seen you got back home?
Why did they take you from Aroostook
into New Brunswick, not crossing where
most cars cross but on an obscure road?

Why did Everett leave the Tobique
Reservation without you, leave you?
Had he fallen out of love with your face
and body somewhere on that journey
from Portland, Maine to New Brunswick?
Had he ceased wanting to kiss and caress
you? What happened he stopped loving

you and your love for him turned to fear?
Why is there a story of a girl running out
of a house naked in the night of a blizzard
running out into a field that must have been
like a vast nowhere, a nocturne nothing
running out naked, the snow falling fast.
Why was she you? What became of you?

My Life Is Not Perfect: Two Enigmas

I

Sue Peterson was shot in the back
of the head in a motel in the Oak Cliff
part of Fort Worth, by Charles Albright,
coincidentally the name of Margie
Albright's dad on *My Little Margie*
starring Gale Storm, who grew up in
Bloomington, which is in the Houston area.
Albright is incarcerated in Big Spring
so this is all Texas, only Sue Peterson
is buried in Alabama. Albright, called
the eyeball killer, gained her trust, he
must have. She was, back in '83,
a street savvy sex worker very familiar
with Oak Cliff. Picture her in a denim
miniskirt, her rump sticking out as
she leans in the passenger window
of a Buick Cutlass, a few other Oak Cliff
girls in heels, like Sue walking that block.
In her mugshot she's stoned. Her eyes,
that he will take for trophies, stare.
Chiseled nose, chin and jaw, a mouth
many might want to stick their tongue in.
One other photo, she's in a living room
in a graduation gown and mortarboard,
her dark hair short in this photo, also
in the one where she's in her little white
ensign cap, and navy blazer. This was
the Seventies. Women officers were less
common than today, far less common.
Gold buttons on the blazer, white shirt,
small black tie kind of like a bow tie.
She must have just gotten out of OCS.
How different in the mugshot, coke
addled, gaunt, circles under her eyes.
Oh, she must have started taking drugs,
got addicted to them and kicked out.

II

There's the film footage: Alexis Arguello
in the ring after he beat BoomBoom Mancini
in a twelve round boxing match. "I love you,
Ray, I love your father." Alexis dripping
sweat, his arm around the warrior
he'd beaten. Typical Arguello, the dark
mustache, the dark hair icicle points
in back down his sweaty neck. He was
nicknamed the explosive thin man.
Outside the ring watching him box
Mancini that night, his beautiful wife.
He may have said to Mancini, after
the fight, your beautiful father. He
had long arms, fast feet, a sharp eye
for what was coming from an opponent.
He retired, and back in his native Nicaragua
got into politics, became disillusioned
with the Sandinistas and the other side
as well. He started taking drugs. One
day, or night, in his home in Managua he
took a loaded pistol, pointed the barrel
to his heart and pulled the trigger.
He was a champion in and out of the ring,
a warrior, the explosive thin man.

Wake

A doughy doll bundled in black sat in
a corner, white hair piled in a Gibson bun.
Pecking her doughy cheek I got a whiff
of withering.
An early night in May. Her husband
lay in the casket, white hair parted
to one side, black rosary beads
in waxen hands. My uncle's hand
on her shoulder. "He's with God."
I wasn't old enough to believe
or disbelieve. To say yes, there is,
or no. Outside, under a canopy
I waited to get into a parked car.

Light Smoker

A light smoker outside a luncheonette,
he stood, feathers of smoke coming up
from the cigarette between his fingers,
taking a break from taking carriages
into the Food Fair. Why not do it again?
I asked. In a round-about way he said no.

"Do it" meant get into the music business,
being recorded, singing in clubs, doing all
he had done to earn a modicum of fame,
the recognition, notoriety that was his,
some eight years before that afternoon
out front of the luncheonette. He didn't want

to go through what it took to get there.
Smoke floated from the cigarette between
his fingers. I thought he didn't because
he was black, I didn't think that then,
but years later. Now I'm not sure. He rode
the bus five days a week to the Food Fair.

On the records his voice, sweet and strong.
He acted that way too, steadfast, reliable.
How much he was drinking about that time
he was taking in carriages, mopping floors,
I'm not sure. Why don't you get back into
the music? No, he lightly shook his head,

stared out into the parking lot at cars,
carriages he would gather and take
in a silver line through automatic doors.
I didn't realize then how young he was,
his early thirties. He wore a white apron.
Food Fair not music was paying the bills.

Scars

I could see the scars on her neck
near her throat, and at the top
of her chest when she wore
a blouse with the collar open.
They were flecks, streaks
that stood out in brightness
in contrast to the dark of her skin.
They were varied in size, some
were jagged. They were not easy
to look at. When I was with her
and my eyes fell on the scars
I looked away,
not wanting her to think I was staring.
She got them in the course of one
night, or day
when the creep she was living with
or had been living with
attacked her with a knife,
almost, I think, slitting her throat.
She had children.
I'd like to think they weren't present
when this human monster
of a husband or maybe only
a boyfriend, lost control,
assuming he ever had control.
How could she have ever gotten
involved with this guy?
Maybe when she met him
he was different. Maybe
she worked at a desk
in an insurance office and one day
a florist's delivery driver came in
and up to her desk with a dozen
red roses.

All I can think of now is the blood
she lost from that attack.
She was lucky to be alive.
She was a student
in my freshman lit class,
and at first I sympathized
with her plight. She needed
extra time to type at the keyboard.

The Long Road from Is to Was

I'm trying to decide what to do with my hair:
let it grow or go back to a flattop. I want
something to offset the jowls I see, when I
look in the mirror. As you age everything
starts to fall, sag, drop toward the ground.
The face muscles included, keep them in
shape, or just let them go, let yourself go.
I don't think so, not if I have any say in it.

Hair more prominent above the forehead,
jowls less noticeable? We'll see, do our best,
resist the wind at our backs that pushes us
forward: don't want to go down that road.
But you must. Okay, going down that road,
I can think too little, or too much, it's like
personal grooming. Some people don't mind
having dirty fingernails, some don't mind

seeing them. I mind, others don't, we're all
different, but everyone's got that long road
ahead, shorter for some, longer for others.
North Maine woods logging roads flanked
by dense evergreens are dirt and they wind.
In some spots impassable even with four-
wheel drive, they get my attention. Imagine
a bunch of Christmas trees growing wild,

and not in a lot outside Walmart or Target. I
drove a long winding road a bit similar only
mine — that stretch from Lubec to Cutler — was
paved. Big difference, but mine too, flanked
by wild trees and brush, eerie in a good way,
had some of that logging road ambiance.
Then, the long road in south New Mexico,
going from Animas to Cloverdale was dirt

and gravel, and sparsely traveled, no traffic
jam on it, or on north Maine logging roads
I saw on film. The gnarly stretch from Lubec
to Cutler I drove often in my '59 Impala
that slowly leaked oil. I wish my friend Lori
in Hawaiian Gardens, California could get
a taste of that road, or the Animus road I
traveled to Cloverdale. She has her roads.

We all have a road, the road we're on now
time traveling from Is to Was. I'd love to
sample those north Maine logging roads.
A film of them is a tease. To be on one, not
just to see but to be on, would be a thrill.
Others might also love that wild solitude, all
those trees. In tall grass a snapping turtle
crawls, its diamond-like black shell,

a shell that comes to points in a pattern of
jagged edges. I saw one on film and years
ago face to face on a riverbank. That shell
makes it distinct. How long does a snapper
live? Is 75 the new 50? I change and am
the same. I have my roads and my road of
minutes, hours, years; spectacular, eerie,
it stretches and winds from Is to Was.

Poolside 1968

A brown hairbrush
sits on a coil of blue towel. A hand
reaches up to the ledge of the pool
in your mother's backyard. Violets
climb the side of a gold porch.
You are gone from summer,
as if off to the war, the Far East,
though that's not what made
your husband a widower.
In red trunks he climbs out of the pool.
Your father is absent, sitting
on the steps out front. Your mother
sitting in the chaise sips a gin rickey.
The widower brushes his hair.
Streaked gray, once it was pure black,
laced with the rice of your wedding.
Your blonde hair cropped,
wind smoothed hairs along wrists
you lifted diving in.
You left no daughters.

To Know, Know, Know Him

He looked shriveled, his long hair looked
like a greasy wig with spikes. Sharp nose
eyes, pinched thin mouth, weak chin.

So different from blonde Lana, prettier
than Marilyn, Marilyn was pretty. Lana
prettier, cornered the blonde beauty thing

that in Hollywood sold tickets. Marilyn
legend, Lana nobody famous, unlike Phil
who wrote "To Know Him Is to Love Him"

and in his digs raised a gun and shot her
dead one night. An accident, Phil maybe
lied to himself, the court, his legal team.

Why did he act in such a way? She walked
through his door but never walked out.
Monster! A dark side friends never saw.

"I knew him but didn't think him capable
of murder," one friend told herself when
Phil in cuffs was led away. As a boy he saw

his father in a parked car shoot himself,
and sometime after wrote the song. No one
knows what goes through another's mind.

How could someone be that dysfunctional,
out of control, evil. Spector was the Wall
of Sound. He created, pushed all the right

buttons. His career a litany of successes.
But he couldn't push the right buttons
in himself. "Just to see him smile makes

my life worthwhile, to know know know him
is to love love love him." Where was all that
the night he took Lana Clarkson's life?

In Church

R.S. Thomas thought television was from
the devil. I can see him at a lectern
in a clapboard church in Wales, railing
at a small congregation not to trifle
with automatic washers and machine-
driven plows. They're from the devil!
Yet R.S. Thomas' poems were questions.
In "In Church" he asks Is this where God
hides from my seeking? In church.

I look at the tiers of stone steps, wide
and light. Behind thick wood doors
the vestibule with a baptismal font.
I enter the church proper. Right above
me, the choir loft, and to my right a fount
of holy water. A vast sea of wood pews.
Up front, on both sides confessionals
with purple velour curtains. Stained glass
depictions of lambs, men in robes, halos.

To the left and right shrines of the Blessed
Virgin. Rows of candles. An altar rail,
more steps, an altar and above it the thick
wood crucifix, Christ crowned in thorns,
a swaddling cloth covers his nakedness.
his palms bloodstained, his eyes look up
toward heaven, I suppose. I liked the smell
of incense from the chalice the priest
used for funerals and mass on holy days.

Isn't every day holy, every virgin blessed?
Two little children kneel in a pew, the church
big and dark, nothing bad happens here.
On a Saturday afternoon a short man
with a bald spot in the crown of his head

parts the velour curtain. The priest pulls
back a slat. The man sees, behind a screen,
a shadow of the priest's face. Bless me.
He confesses to the priest his sins.

An early Wednesday morning two Sisters
of Charity, in long black gowns, their faces
framed in white squared boarders, so not
even one strand of hair is showing, kneel
in a pew. Sister John, whose face is long
and thin, with a Roman nose, puts her hand
over Sister Gerard's. Both are young.
Sister Gerard, her chin stubbled with acne,
kisses Sister John's long smooth hand.

They are the only ones there, hanging
from the waists of both nuns, long strings
of black beads, with small silver crosses,
Christ on the Cross, who, like the Christ
above the altar, sees everything. Is this
the place where God hides? Is He there
behind the confessional's screen. What are
your sins? Or around a vestibule corner,
or in the halo of the bearded brown robe,

St. Francis with a lamb on his shoulder?
His eyes look upward. Is this the place
where I hide from God? In church. One
of those two children, the boy Clifford,
sobbed when Sister Margaret asked him
Where is your father? My father's dead.
That wasn't in church. Church is where God
hides, maybe up in the choir loft. I wish
I were like R.S. Thomas, pure poetry.

Lady

She's corgi. Mom had her since a puppy.
My mom, Willett, went into Cresthaven, she
couldn't keep her. Is there a newsletter?
Oh, a webpage. If you could put up Lady's
picture. She is a sweetie. I think Lady was
the only one Willett knew towards the end.
Cresthaven didn't allow dogs, so Willett
couldn't have her. We have her in a crate

in the foyer off the kitchen. Sam and I,
we have two teens, we're out all day and
Lady's fine. She's seventeen. Oh, a place
in Weatherford takes seniors. That's a drive
from Ozona. Like you, I'm out showing
properties. Sam's on call with Texas Power.
The kids with their activities, Michelle's
in band. Maybe your webpage. Lady's

a sweetheart. Willett, people used to say,
she is just like your child. We had dogs
growing up in Witchita Falls. No, we can't
keep her. That's out of the question.
A shelter here in Ozona. I hadn't known.
That would be better than taking her
out and dropping her in the Sandhills.
We can't keep her. Sam has allergies.

Michelle had a hamster but she's not much
into animals, nor is Mike, our son. Maybe
someone at the shelter — I didn't know
there is one. It's overcrowded? Someone
maybe will drive her to that place in
Weatherford. My uncle had a dog got lost.
The pound called and my uncle told
the pound, That dog is old. Put it to sleep.

Reciprocity

I want a can opener that has a beak
like a hawk's, that I can push into the lid
of a can of pineapple juice, and see
the hollow triangle like an upside down
baseball diamond.
I want a chimney, a path through elms,
a negligee pinup, and a smoking jacket
that's silk and lightly padded and has
little diamond-shaped patterns, a lapel
with long curves, and a silk belt that goes
through loops, that I can either leave
hanging loose or tie. I want a picture of
Rita Haworth in a pillbox with a veil
that falls past the bridge of her nose.

If you help me get what I want I'll help
you, Ethel, one of the dead,
cold in your grave, wanting everything.
The yellow eggcup you made in the shape
of a duck has green wings. Its webs and bill,
a light orange. It's on my sill.
As you primp your permed hair in a mirror
in your brick house on a hill,
I could gather orange and grapefruit rinds
to bring to your compost, I could wax
your green Plymouth. I saw your husband's
mother, but never yours.
Did you live in a house on a hill after you
moved from the house I remember?
You picked me up from school one day
in your Plymouth. Its interior, light gray
smelled damp. I could put an egg
in the cup you baked in a kiln.

The Dating Game

Rod Necessary, pleasure to meet you,
or Rod Necessary, the pleasure is mine.
Never Rodney, what my mother named me.
After the theme tune, part Monkees, part
Here's Johnny, I heard bachelor number 3
Rodney Necessary. In polished loafers,
navy blue blazer, the collar of my lime
shirt spread over the lapel, I walked on
stage and took my place, dark waves of
lustrous hair falling past my shoulders.

Like others, I was a referral, my accountant,
who'd been on tv's *The Dating Game*.
When he's not on a surfboard in Santa
Monica or riding his motorcycle or camped
out in the mountainous desert of Warner
Springs Rodney is a studio photographer.
I smiled at the audience. Bachelor 3,
if you were a food, what food would you be?
A banana. You could peel me later. What
is your favorite time? Night, it's so alive

with sensuous mystery. A fine arts degree
from UCLA, a passing acquaintance with
Harry Callahan, I cooked Mediterranean
dishes, grew roses. My Italian loafers and
manicured nails cinched me as her choice.
The audience loved me! Yet afterwards,
a fluke made me not her choice to go out,
something behind my eyes. No red rose at
an opened door for her! Smart girl. Like
the one I picked up on the beach and drove

75 miles into the mountainous desert to
photo shoot, and rape, the girl who said
yes sir, no sir, talkative. I let her out to use
a gas station's Ladies, the next thing I'm
in cuffs. My mother put up ten thousand
bail and I was set free . . . to rape and kill
Penny Williams, Cheryl Michaels, Barbara
Heidi, to name a few. I remember names,
and mementos: panties, nylon stockings,
the 11-year-old Theresa Riley I got in my car

and in a room strangled, screwed, and taken
out to a landfill. *The Dating Game.* My long
dark wavy hair made me a cinch to win.
I never watched it in my cell or in the rec
area. Lying on my cot I saw eyes of corpses
stare past me, at nothing. Now I'm no one,
nothing, a nightmare memory to ones at my
trial. I didn't fry in the yellow mama
or get a needle's goodnight kiss. Bachelor
number 3, What's your favorite time? Night.

Schaeffer Wonders

This accident from 1965 astonishes
Schaeffer. He writes: I am far away,
but I can see the broad boulevard,
the side streets of my hometown,
and can imagine the Davis car blows
thoughtless through the Stop and slams

the tail end of the Edwards car so it
spins a quick whirlwind on this Sunday
night of light traffic. Lethal turbulence
in this time before seatbelts flings
Mr. Edwards from behind the wheel out
to the street. His head dashes the curb.

He was going from his house to Lucille
Desadario's, a two-mile drive. Lucile sat
between Mr. Edwards and Chris, his son.
Both passengers in shock on the leather
front bench, the gold sedan's spinning
stops. Still as death, that intersection.

I can hear sirens, see two patrol cars on
the scene. A yellow ambulance's red top
whirls in the still night. A badge, his back
to the ambulance, jots with a pen in
a pad. The ambulance's back door opens.
The sheeted dead man is lifted in.

I wonder if Lucille, that night, wore shorts,
sandals, a thin gold cross on a chain
and, if so, at what hour she unhooked
the chain's clasp. I wonder if a red and white
box of Marlboros fell from the dash
onto the floorboard, Chris's cigarettes.

He reaches for one and with a Zippo
lights it. Its orange tip glows in the dark
as the badge jots with a ballpoint.

The ambulance leaves the boulevard.
Chris and Lucille leave, and John Davis,
the other driver. I remember Mr. Edwards

dove perfectly off a high board,
arrow-straight into a pool of blue water
rippled with sun rings. Iron-gray hair,
tall and straight, at 47 still athletic
when he walked out the door with
car keys in hand, that Sunday night.

Topsy

My dark side isn't as dark as Thomas
Edison's. Edison gave us light,
and for that like any sane person
I'm down on my knees thanking him.
But what about Topsy the elephant?
A barker or some such shoved a lit
smoke, the orange tip up Topsy's trunk
and Topsy hurt the barker,
crushed his foot or just sprained his foot.
For that Topsy, outside a tent, chained
standing but immobile,
got electric bolts shot through her.
She was wired, it's on YouTube, smoke
rising, the elephant's ponderous fall,
all because Edison tried something out.
Afterwards he celebrated the execution,
broke out the champagne.
Hooray for advancement!
He shook hands with circus higher ups
and ones who did the dark work.

Autobiography

An autobiography of a lizard should contain
lizard reflections: reminiscences, confessions
daydreams. One morning the lizard said,
"All right, Uncle Baxter, I'll get my stuff."
The next moment, perched on Uncle Baxter's
shoulder, the lizard watched as Uncle Baxter
handled a crane; a big ball on a chain
crumbled a stone wall. Then there was the time
the lizard and Uncle Baxter relaxed at St. Kitts
in palm shade, a view of turquoise water,
Uncle Baxter in a lounge, tall green drink
in hand, lost in *War and Peace;* the lizard
slithered along motes of a sandcastle kids
had built then abandoned. An autobiography
of a lizard should contain the lizard's preferred
bowling team, its preferred soup and rainforest.
Uncle Baxter had a German Shepherd, Lucky,
the lizard didn't like; when the lizard, crossing
a room, made eye contact with the dog
it looked like it wanted to kill him. The lizard
lived across the street from Uncle Baxter.
When Lucky got old, Uncle Baxter helped
the dog up the stairs. That ended. Uncle
was sad but the lizard couldn't share in that.
Uncle was alone in that dark hour, smoking
a cigarette, looking out a window. One day
Uncle Baxter took the lizard into the city of neon
lights, names on marquees, honking taxi cabs.
Messengers in long coats scuttled across
an avenue. The lizard wondered what they
were delivering, what was in the messages.
Another day Uncle Baxter took the lizard
to a place of rocks and shadows, and
shouted something only the lizard could hear.
There was no one around, no one for miles.

Sweet Seasons

Lizard asked Uncle Baxter about Marilyn
Kilroy.
She was born in Savannah, Georgia
in 1927 and died in New York City in 1969.
Who was she?

A torch singer, but one song of hers,
Laffin at Me, sounds like typical pop schlock
you'd hear from the late fifties.
How did she make her mark?
In '51 she appeared in *The Big Night,*

the one unflawed character in this film
about the corruption of life in America
as it was as opposed to how it is.
She was the one George, the protagonist,
looked at and said to, you're so beautiful

even though . . . his inference
was even though you are black. You saw
the change in her face, at first
pleased, suddenly revolted.
What did she look like?

She had brown eyes. The features in her
face perfectly proportioned,
she was lovely, but not uncommonly so.
What else about her do you know?
She sang in New York clubs. In November

1969 she and her twenty year old
stepdaughter were murdered in their
apartment because her husband Pat
Jackson, a car salesperson, had failed
to pay a debt he owed to drug dealers.

Did she herself do drugs?
I have no idea. She may have. I only know
she sang, and acted in a few films.
She sang in *The Big Night* moments before
George sidled up to her.

She was the impetus for racism as an
integral part of the corruption depicted
in this film, which, unlike Laffin at Me,
was not dollar-driven but had something
to say, and to show, the face of Terry

Angelus, played by Marilyn, aka Mauri
Leighton, who in real life was murdered,
either shot, stabbed, or beaten,
I don't know how, there's much I don't know.
I saw her face change as she stood

outside the club in that movie, about
to go someplace else, shortly after midnight,
I don't know where. You see
George leave in a cab with his pal
the professor, you don't see Terry again.

You know she's in *The Big Night*
not only for her singing.
Were drugs rampant in New York in '69?
I suspect so. Marilyn's stage name
was Mauri Leighton. She was beautiful.

Humpback

When I was a little kid, my friend's father
had a stash of girlie magazines with all
these beautiful centerfolds. Yet he himself
was humpbacked. I'd see him, as I am now,
in my mind, and seeing his humped back
I instinctively want to turn away. He kept
the girlies in a cubbyhole, off the bathroom.
His stash of lust: *Dude, Nugget, Daddy,
Uncut, Handjobs, Kingsize, Sex Life.* All
we did was look; this was before puberty.

He wore a grease-monkey suit, he owned
an auto upholstery shop, he was Polish,
his name was Adolph. The suit was dull
silver with dull blue lines I see up around
his humped back, blue lines that splayed
out like finite fishbones, of fish fossils
embedded in rock from prehistoric times.
His egg head, bald on top, flat in back,
must have been crammed with cleavages,
that deep line between breasts he fondled,

kissed, sucked and bit while jacking off.
Nothing wrong with that. He was married,
had two kids and a successful business.
He lived in a house on a hill, wore dark-
framed glasses. His skin was light brown,
even his bald head, wisps of black hair
on the sides. His face, wide and drawn,
seldom smiled. Though he was outgoing,
inside he was private, the Adolph even
his wife, Adele, didn't see, is my thought.

No one around, he visited pics of girls
buxom, hot to trot during the Cold War.
He stroked to a pic in *Sin:* a young woman
knelt, her mouth around a big hard cock
and cum dripping, the private Adolph.
The Sundays he went to mass were rare,
but he did go. I'm not sure if he walked
a path in woods that led to the river
and stood on the riverbank and looked
at the weeping willow on the other side,

the most beautiful tree I've ever seen
that wasn't in a photograph. I wonder if
he ever saw it. He was always working,
either at his shop, stitching upholstery,
needle in hand, or at home, a hammer,
a saw, or the spirit level — dull silver,
like a heavy ruler, in the center a yellow
liquid bubble — he used to build shelves.
He spoke in low spurts, like snores.
The women in his girlie stash loved him.

St. Francis

Katie Zwerling, leave everything behind
and come with me to St. Francis,
a little town way up in Maine, way up
there, way out there. When people say
out in the middle of nowhere they mean
this place, surrounded by logging roads

cleared a hundred years ago so trucks
could haul logs to populated places.
You've seen roads surrounded by trees.
These roads are really surrounded by trees!
You drive on, it's a bit scary. Nothing's
around these winding dirt roads but trees

and this town, where we could settle
in a house with heat, air conditioning.
Would the house have central air? Maybe.
But it would have electricity, plumbing,
and we'd be close to the logging roads,
get to know them so we wouldn't get stuck

or lost. People want to be near the ocean,
or a lake or a golf course. I'd take these
logging roads any day over a golf course
or a mall, roads with trees around, pines,
evergreens, no vehicles, except us in ours,
my jeep with a GPS, so as not to get lost.

So much snow in winter, a snowmobile
would be needed. I could buy one!
Snowsuits to keep us warm. Go out
on those roads, not too far, and come back
to our house in St. Francis. Both of us
stripped naked I could kiss you all over.

We could make love, then go to a local cafe,
come home, watch *Reign* on Netflix.
St. Francis has WiFi. We could call people
on our cell phones. When logging roads
were made, did they have telephones way up
there? It's way, way different from here.

The Great Billy Williams

When I was a little kid there was this pop
song, "I'm Gonna Write Myself a Letter."
I remember hearing it in a bar, on a jukebox,

some drunk guy singing along,
like lightly slamming the open palm of his hand
on the bar in time to the jaunty rhythms.

Well, it was just a song, kind of catchy, but I
didn't think much of it. The bar, the building
itself was wooden, and in a low valley,

between one steep hill and a lower hill.
By the mid-sixties it was torn down and
replaced by a small brick strip mall.

But this song was a big hit, and the guy
singing, his voice sounded kind of cranky.
"Gonna write myself a letter,

make believe it came from you, oh yeah!"
Just another song. When I got to my teens,
I bought a 45 disc, "I Don't Wear My Heart

on My Sleeve" by the Charioteers. A ballad,
the lead's male alto was high-pitched and very
smooth. Elegant. I loved it, love it still.

Fast forward to me in my fifties. I got
a Charioteers CD and realized this alto lead,
singing ballads and up-tempo tunes like

"Way Down Yonder in New Orleans" was
the same guy who, back in the fifties,
had this one smash hit. On "Letter"

his voice didn't sound high and smooth like
on the ballads. I was astounded to learn
they were one in the same, Billy Williams.

I purchased the CD from a record shop by
mail. I talked to the shop owner, now
deceased, and he said Billy Williams

was a pretty good singer. He sure was!
A very good singer. He made other pop
things but also a lot of pretty great music.

You listen to him on "So Long," really listen,
and you know you've been someplace.
So smooth, so sad it's sadness

pushed to the limits of joy, pure joy.
The sound of a singer in love with what he's
singing. A master. A blend of passion

and control. He did enough of that, over
and over, to where he went beyond good,
to greatness. Billy Williams, a great singer,

I read somewhere, ended up living in
a basement, on the fringe of homeless.
He needs some credit, though

he's long dead and it won't matter to him,
but as Frost said, "The fact
is the sweetest dream labor knows."

The truth is in the sound of the smooth alto
that is Billy Williams, alto lead
of the Charioteers, the great Billy Williams.

The Weather

Ed Book, one of the crew on *Tim Peeples
in the Morning,* wasn't on every morning,
but this particular one he was. There was
Clair Sims doing the weather and Tim
asked Ed what he was thinking.

"I'm wondering what Clair looks like naked."
Clair, pretty but more handsome, shiny
lustrous dark brown hair, brown eyes in
a wide nicely shaped face, pretty mouth
strong chin seemed only slightly flustered.

"It's not a pretty sight," her come back,
got a chuckle from the two men. Clair
wasn't small, didn't look small on TV. Big-
boned, not hulking but curvy, like she'd
played sports in high school and college,

curvy in her hips and butt, with sumptuous
firm breasts, handsome, and undeniably
sexy. Not a pretty sight, her comeback,
spot on. Cool, she stood her ground, didn't
storm off set, continued the weather.

What would Ed have done had someone,
while he was on camera, said the same
to him? What would anyone have done?
His remark so sudden. I admit I liked it,
the thought of Clair naked . . . she had a body,

well, it's not hard to think men and women
lusted after her body, that went well with
her strong delicate jaw, dark eyes and hair.
"What Clair looks like" . . . candid, thoughtless.
Her eyes showed she didn't like it. Maybe

right after, Ed regretted what he said.
But Tim Peebles' chuckle hinted he too
wondered what Clair looked like naked.
What do I myself look like? My swarthy
body with no clothes to mask who I am.

Mai

Tet, 1968:

In the morning light, the dead
in a grated clearing at the edge
of rice paddies.
The Danang
Security guards in the open back of a truck
passing quickly
the dead stacked in rows.
Laid out like piles of laundry,
lifeless in green fatigues,
I thought 500,
that only 24 hours before were soldiers.
And wonder
what brought them into the night
rice paddies?
Did each choose to be there?
As I chose
to stand watch
in the city, to guard an admiral's quarters
to stand on
a rooftop as the sky lit with flares.
The admiral in robe and slippers,
smoking a cigar. Like his guards
unaware of the firefight
in the paddies, across the river from the city.
I remember
the heard and felt thuds, the sky bursts
of flares. Eventually
he left the rooftop for his bedroom.
At sunrise the truck came and collected us.
I remember
the rice paddies' tall grass.
In its foreground the grated clearing,
a southwest corner.
In daylight a paved intersection busy
with traffic.
Across the street, the northwest corner's
tower in which, months before Tet
I stood watch.

At the base of the tower one day
Mai, ten years old
held the hand of her baby sister, Huong.
With Mai I traded
a sandwich I'd bought from a vendor
for her picture, which I have in an album.
The sandwich I thought pork
or ham, likely dog meat.
The sandwich
wrapped in newspapers in Mai's hand
as she walked away.
She and Huong in loose blouses and slacks
light colored, rumpled
like cotton pajamas,
came and went from the base of the tower.
I remember the rice paddies,
the intersection, afternoons
a Quan Chan in smart fatigues,
polished boots, a red scarf and white
gloves, with a whistle directed traffic.
His dark helmet
with white letters QC on front. Pivoting
his body, moving his hands,
like a ballet.
Whichever QC happened to be there,
moving
gracefully, precisely, in stark contrast
to the dead soldiers
I saw as the truck passed
the bodies
stacked in rows, the soldiers
dying the night before, while
I stood on the admiral's roof
and Mai slept
or maybe huddled in a corner with Huong
in a house not far from the fighting,
the killing and being killed.
In Mai's picture she's in a studio gazebo.
If she's still living . . . what became of her?

Schaeffer and Sheila

How sad when your son dies and you lose
the will to have sex, almost the will to live.
Someone I know. I don't mean
to sound cold. Sheila and I met on line.
Soon she's telling me she loves me.
Are you nuts, I thought; you don't know me,
you're making declarations of love.
What? From a few pictures, a few words.

She retired and moved to the mountains,
where she'd wanted to be. Then her son
and his wife moved in with her. When we met,
only online, she was wishing them gone
so she could enjoy her home in peace.
I got the impression they were meth heads:
Deanna a convenience store clerk,
Rick, good with electrical stuff, didn't work.

Freeloaders, I thought, and used that word
more than once. She said maybe
they'd buy a trailer her brother owned. No.
She bitched about their being with her,
also about missing jewelry and money.
Meth heads, I never said that to her
but to myself. Then Rick died in his sleep.
Mother and son, they'd never been apart.

Sex talk stopped, and love declarations.
I didn't mind; it was online, going nowhere.
Even if Rick hadn't died the chance Sheila
and I would ever get together, "get it on,"
was very slim. I never said I love you back.
When she said it I felt irked, annoyed, but
never told her that. The sex talk was good
for a while, my feeling she wanted me.

Then Rick died. Not having a son myself
I couldn't plug into her grief, I imagine
its depth, but can't feel it. I only know
while Rick was in her home with his wife
she mentioned missing jewelry and money.
Freeloaders, thieves. All her adult life
it had always been she and Rick, now he
was gone, and her sex drive. Her will to live?

The Pearls

I look out and see the long flat strip
of land that diminishes. Earth meets sky.
Empty. I've come to like it out here. The air
base, where World War II pilots trained,
used only for gliders now. On its far end,
across the airbase, a prison they were just
starting work on when you were here.

Here is flat and there are no trees, nothing
like the winding roads of the north Louisiana
you came from, or the green woodsy hills
part of Tennessee where you are. For a time
you were here, with the metal buildings and
no trees, no water to speak of, lakes, well,
there's a small artificial one, and a pond

out by the airbase, where, when you were
here, we walked dogs that have been gone
for years. A few nights back, driving home
from a jazz concert I detoured onto a road
that goes past the park with the pond and
came to a T, and thought to turn right but it
was so incredibly dark when I looked right

I told myself that's too dark for me. Anyway
it just leads to an iron gate they put up to
keep people from driving down onto the air
base. I turned left. That darkness was like
no darkness I'd ever seen. Don't go there, I
told myself. But there was another time,
late afternoon, Christmas Eve, I went out

walking on the airbase, the same long strip
where we had walked dogs. Only this late
afternoon I was alone and the air was quite
foggy. I had a portable device that let me
listen to CDs one disc at a time, and on it
this one CD of Jelly Roll Morton, it's called
The Pearls, a ballad about a woman

who went to prison for killing another
woman (over a man), and what happened
to her when she got there. Her message is,
Be a good girl and wear the pearls,
a ballad of regret, sung, told by Jelly Roll
who plays piano as he tells her story. It was
very foggy as I walked the long air strip

listening to that music that Christmas Eve,
with her story adding up to, it wasn't worth
it. He wasn't worth it, that man, not worth
going to prison for. The next day, Christmas
we had an ice storm; it was so slippery I
couldn't even step outside and walk around.
But before the ice settled, early morning,

I was able to get my dog Jesse — do you
remember her, the Wheaton? — and ride
around town a short while in my red truck.
The ice was just starting. We rode around
town maybe twenty minutes, this town of
flat roads, few trees, but we didn't go by
the airbase. By then they'd built the prison.

Sext

Mel Steinhaus owns all three *Fifty Shades
of Grey* films, and skydives,
the first dive two years after her stroke.
One Saturday night, on a love seat
I sexted Mel. She loved to sext.
Once she sexted about when she worked
at Walmart. There shopping with her
first husband, in Employees Only
she went down on her co-worker lover,
then kissed her husband
as her lover watched from afar.
That Sunday, on campus in my office
grading papers, I got a text from Joe,
Mr. Steinhaus. Mel is in the hospital.
She wanted you to know.
She loved to sext, in a second sexting
stopped. A year later she and Joe
entered La Fiesta. I rose from the booth.
Joe and I shook hands. I'd heard about
him. Here he was, a string bean,
sallow cheeks, frayed ball cap, blonde,
blue-eyed like Mel. She limped
stiffly. I hadn't seen her in many years.
Not the vibrant single mother
in my freshman lit class, her face
puffed, splotchy red, her body forever
unshapely, like a box.
They were in Clovis to visit her mom,
they'd driven from Nebraska.
In a recent text, she said in La Fiesta
I didn't even kiss her. What do you want,
me to jump up and stick my tongue
in your mouth in front of your husband?

Voices from the Past

Voices from the past.
Close your eyes and listen.
*When I leave this house
my time isn't my own,*
says the bald man.
We were going to go to Florida,
says the woman in the shade.
You can move to Russia,
rasps a third voice.
I've only had three beers,
says another, long distance.
And from her nursing home
corner bed, *Proud of you.*
Their words, now mine,
as you have your bits of truth,
like black beads, each
bead a year, an occasion,
the many occasions a necklace.
You wear a circle of truth,
these voices at odd moments
and moments not odd.
New Year's Eve, the living room
couch, midnight, hands
over my eyes, I hear them,
my parents who died last year.

Toddle

You can tell me but I'll never know
how you felt the moment your son
stood on his own and toddled away
from and then back to you

on the S shaped walk near porch
jalousies and a spruce's shade
that spilled into the walk he walked
up and down. Happy, a little sad?

His mouth had sucked your nipple
his first days, then that sunny day
outside the house you rented he
stepped away. Baby's first steps.

Your only son, his hair dark like yours
and his two older sisters'. A time
when, your marriage crumbling,
Jason Tyler followed you past pool

tables and turned a narrow corner.
In a stall in the Ladies you straddled
his lap, faster, harder. Only he
heard you moan, whimper, climaxing.

Jason, blond like your husband, like
your husband, rode a Harley. Unlike
you, he came from money, his family
Tyler Electric. Last time you two spoke

was the A&P. You put a yellow,
black Chock Full o' Nuts tin in your cart,
looked up and there he was, tall in
a long dark coat, long hair straggly,

eyes red, a Sunday morning hangover.
You said, "I'm in nursing school." And
he, "That's great." By the time your son
was in the first grade you were single,

a nurse, on your shift the morning
Jason spilled from his Harley on Henley
Road. He lay on the macadam lot of
Stargher's, with its tinted glass, that sold

smoked meats. A bystander
held his hand, praying as he left her.
Your son Frank recently married.
He's not ready for children, you said.

I wonder if anyone is ever ready.

Extra Duty

There was a name for it; that was the name.
It was as if in his lanky frame, shoulders
hunched, eyes downcast, in his big hands
he'd cupped a nest-like house he'd built
from toothpicks, and from his mouth, (he
always twirled a small toothpick), he'd said
"This is structure, I'm giving this gift to you
tonight in this warehouse with its office
to the south and light through office
windows, as tiles gleam wet on the office
deck you've swabbed, I'm showing you
what my hands have made and cup, this
structure I'm giving you so you'll have it
after you leave this office and warehouse."

How fortunate I was, to one day, months
before that night with light through windows
and the dark office tiles wet from the swab,
how fortune I was to walk through a door
and report to him, and work stacking boxes,
shelving small items, answering to him,
he answered to Chief Alvarez who answered
to Lieutenant JG Cutter. We had structure,
a hierarchy, but Brown that night gave me
a structure, not a house of toothpicks but
of events that comprised his life, for that's
what he gave me, though I didn't know it
that night, in all the days I answered to him.

Last I saw him was in the compartment of
the LPH I was on after I'd gotten back from
a year of shore duty in Vietnam. No longer
was I working for Brown, Roland K, first
class petty officer. Like me he was assigned
a ship. We visited down in a compartment
of mine, on the LPH. I never heard his voice

after that day. But I remember distinctly
his low deep voice, that I'd heard every day
in the warehouse, more than once he said
not to give the civilians anything extra. He
twirled a toothpick, a lanky light-skinned
Black sailor. He indeed was Black, indeed
a sailor who'd enlisted before Civil Rights
and did little more than paint bulkheads
and swab decks in years before he became
the First Class I was assigned to work for.

He seldom looked me in the eye when he
talked, most often telling me to do things,
but he talked straight and that one night
I and one other seaman swabbed the tiles
he talked of swabbing and painting, only
a little, enough for us to know who he was,
what he'd been though, (no regret, no self
pity at all in his voice), only I knew because
he spoke clearly. Had I asked, Were you
discriminated against because of color?
I don't know what he would have said,
maybe nothing, very possibly nothing, or
he might have changed the subject.

Black Menace

Sonny Liston picked cotton,
endured welts from his father's strap,
hitchhiked from Arkansas to St. Louis
to live with his mother,
dropped out of school, stole a cantaloupe
from a vender, sat in a paddy-wagon,
sparred in a ring, hit hard.
A belt with the big gold buckle signified
he was the baddest man on the planet.
Got ticketed by a cop for driving out
the entrance of a MacDonald's,
fired a pistol at Cassius Clay who ran
out of there so fast at a press conference,
got beaten by Clay in the ring, trained
hard on the heavy bag, the speed bag
jumped rope, jogged, and in the ring
got knocked down by Muhammad Ali,
who retained the title Sonny lost
in their first fight. Had massive biceps
chest and shoulders, wore a sharkskin
suit a pork pie hat a pencil thin mustache.
Leaned down and smiled at a little white
boy who was smiling at him and shook
the boy's hand. In a park, arrested
for loitering, cops harassed him like
they'd done all his life, even after he was
champion. Bag man for the mob
he stepped behind a counter and grabbed
a bookie hard by the collar in Las Vegas,
where his wife, having been gone two
days, came home and found him dead.
Slumped and swollen. Give him credit.
He laughed and smiled. Those who knew
him saw a man different from his public self.

The Glorious Present

I folded my sweatpants into a pillow
so he had his own and would stop
taking mine
as we lay in bed side by side.
I woke in the middle of the night,
looked at him asleep on his pillow.
A small joy jolted through me.
When he passes on
I'm going to know what being alone
means. I'll go to a solitary place
and weep. The greatest tears are
the tears we don't cry. I'll tell you
I am without him. However
this dog, who found me,
whom I found six years ago, my half
spaniel who chases ducks into
water, is here, sniffing grass as I
sit in a chair on a patio.
As you are with your bulldog
Tommy, I'm with Sherlock.

Aroostook

One night, standing in an open door,
looking out at the dark I daydreamed
about being in Aroostook, the County.
I was in the American Southwest. Aroostook
is way up in the Northeast, about as east
as a person can go and still be in the States.

I don't know what started my Sunday night
Aroostook daydream. Only I thought
Aroostook way up there out of the way,
which meant few people, and fewer wanted
to go there. I guess I wanted to feel special,
like no one wanted to go there but me.

Nothing there that I didn't have here except
lots of snow. I'm not a snow fan, I wanted
to be there in summer, maybe the one time
no snow falls on Allagash and Bridgewater.
How do these towns differ? Go and see.
I thought about it but I had papers to grade,

bills to pay, promises to keep. I couldn't
just pack up my Ford 150, stuffing
suitcases in the camper shell and drive
all the way up there. Though it's possible.
Though I'd be fired from my school where
I teach English and students at desks play

with their phones, which they likely do
in New Limerick and Westmanland,
assuming they have schools, maybe
churches. What would it be like praying
in a church in Blaine, or buying stamps in
St. Agatha's post office, if it has one?

I Googled a page of Aroostook's towns and
plantations. What, in 2020, is a plantation?
They are there, according to Google. I had
them memorized and thought about them.
I wanted to walk through a door in
Frenchville, to get out of a car in Mars Hill.

The Invisible Man Plants a Kiss on the Forehead of Absence

The invisible man
likes ornate postage stamps
stamps with rivers, ferns, crowns
and magpies. The invisible man
likes roses on stamps, and steps
and balconies and courtyards.

He likes tents, whips, milk boxes
dead end streets, fire escapes
cobbled hilly streets and a garden
with white trellises and stone benches
along a river bend. He likes things
he's seen and touched, and places
he's been to and will never be in again.

He knows people who like some
of the things he likes. One wears
a gray coat, another a bow tie
and a watch fob. Like him, they
walk quiet streets, and look
at wind in treetops. No one asks
why he thinks of himself as invisible.
He doesn't know why. As for absence
he kisses that forehead every day.

George and the Dobermans

George's Majestic Lounge
was more tempestuous than majestic.
George's hobby was yelling.
As waitresses
swung through doors in and out the kitchen,
their arms stacked with plates,
he couldn't help rush them. Schaeffer,
there days, part-time,
liked finding silver when he cleaned
under the bar. With him
George was terse but not hysterical.
A disgruntled 5'9, salt and pepper hair,
wire rim glasses, he yelled
so it was a wonder the waitresses,
for the most, kept cool.
No waiters worked there.
Schaeffer guessed the majestic part
happened at night.
Early one Saturday Schaeffer
walked George and his wife's two ancient
Dobermans down a dark alley
behind the Majestic.
Their rickety legs creaked over ice,
their snouts sniffed cold asphalt.
Schaeffer felt uneasy. What if something
were to happen?
George was always looking for a fight.

Sunbeams

When the Sunbeams sing "Please Say
You'll Be Mine" at the end they pause
a second then in harmony sing "you are
the one for me." How I felt about you.

In my room the gray wallpaper's campfire
patterns — you were the flame, the curve
in the river out my window, treetops' green,
wooded paths, chimneys' bricks, rusted

stones in the Revolutionary War graveyard
across the road from the Little League field,
south end of town. You were the circle
outside the tall columns of the high school

before men on scaffolds wrought a wing.
You were clouds above the river and light
in the morning, light in your eyes, light
in your long dark hair. Body and soul a girl.

The girl. In Glory you can't hear me.
I look from glass at river's sweeping curve,
and see your hair your face your body,
all of you beautiful, as you are, as you are.

Abandoned Tenements

I lose the insomnia contest.
Someone stays awake the longest
who looks like but is not yours
truly. In a drawing contest I draw despair
as walls of black windows, hollow space.
Crossing the street I step up my pace
in the contest to see who leaves wins.
I stay on the street abandoned,
not wondering where did they go,
only mesmerized by the dark hollows
that were windows people looked out.
The next contest, to see who's proud.
Yet I'm fixated on the empty street,
abandoned tenements, summer heat.

Eleven Roses

The eleven roses and the twelfth is you
jingle,
checks in the sport coat of Pinky Lee,
a mumble-jumble
of high feelings
in the evangelist's pompadour,
we were ornate
as a Fabergé egg under glass,
happy as perch in the Hook River.
Daydreams,
gum balls, Caladryl
cured our ills.
Whether water skiing
or nursing a scotch & milk, all of us
kept Hoover's *Masters of Deceit*
bookmarked
for bedtime reading.
It was mind boggling.
"Take that,"
said Pete the grocer.
We shot marbles.
We emulated mobster Frank Costello,
desired *Knots Landing's*
Abby Cunningham.
"Calypso Boogie"
blared in
"the penny candy store beyond the el."
We sipped
white port and lemon juice
and found eggs in a robin's nest.

Philip

Schaeffer texts Tasia:

I told him to tether his dog to the back
bumper of my truck, so he did. Then
the four of us went upstairs
to my apartment, at Woodleaf, had
a drink and recapped our weekend.

I should have said, "Bring your dog up."
I didn't think, yeah, your pet's out there.
It could be snatched by a tweaker,
or, worse, a human monster dog fighter.

No wonder we haven't talked. Could have,
should have. What's done is done.
I could reach out, ask for forgiveness
still, the ill feelings are there, seeds

of my thoughtlessness that afternoon.
So I won't reach out, what's done
can't be undone, and I've no urge
to plant, what? The seeds of healing.

I screwed up. Please forgive me
I could say. I've no urge to go back,
like an AA member, going down a list
of lives he or she made miserable
while in an alcohol rage or stupor.

At that time, my decade in Woodleaf
a dog, or any pet was simply a thing
not a creature dependent on humans.
"Bring him up." It had been kenneled

all weekend. What an ass I was!
But no one said anything, no one said
I'd regret that Woodleaf moment
and others, other places. Tethered,
the dog waited for him to come down.

Tennis Court 1958

As palm fronds sway in the sky a net
divides players paid, as I am, to be here.
One player lifts a racquet
and serves a ball, it bounces shear
off a shield invisible back to the server.

Similarly Colgate's Gardol shields
our teeth from decay,
its protective coat God-
like, like the Diety. God isn't chemistry,
Gardol (sodium lauroyl), or a windy day

in a commercial for tooth cream.
I stand in the foreground in tennis whites.
Brush with Colgate.
What is God? God shield us from harm.

Visitations from the Other Side

Months before the sudden death that sent
him, or rather transformed him, all he was,
into ashes scattered in his sister's garden,
where his mother's ashes are, he told me
of the eye operation on both eyes that let
him know finally how great it was to see

clearly. Ever since childhood he'd seen
through coke-bottle lenses; then all that
suddenly changed. Last I saw him was I
think outside an Italian restaurant, maybe,
the morning after, getting into his SUV
in the lot of a four-story condo complex,

this person whose crude penmanship on
a small white envelope in my mind's eye
I see this early morning. Memory is tricky.
I can't recall, was it the restaurant or SUV,
my last look at him? But I do recall one
afternoon I looked out a kitchen window

of the small communal house I lived in
when you used to visit. I looked down at
your sleeping face, bowled over by beauty
that was yours, your closed eyes, lustrous
dark lashes as you slept in morning light.
That afternoon I was not expecting him,

how happy I was to look out that window
and see the coke-bottle lenses that were
part of him, the small nose and mouth set
in the broad face that, with gristly hair,
made him look like a lion, he'd had that look
even when his hair was short, in his teens.

He was walking along the side of the house
nearer to Dinkytown. I don't know if that
was north or south, only, I'm certain, he was
on the side nearer to Dinkytown: Varsity
Theater, Russoff's Bookshop, Savaron's
Bookshop, Sammy D's, Valli Pizza where

you and I sat in a booth one Monday night
with snow falling outside. I lived in a big
white house on a corner, then. But when I
saw him that afternoon I motioned to him
through the glass and the next moment he
was standing right in front of me. I do not

remember that moment. He'd hitched
rides to Minneapolis and had my address.
I looked out the kitchen window, saw him
walking along the side of that house. I recall
your sleeping face, your navy blue parka
lying in the chair in my basement room.

He may have slept there, but more likely
crashed on the living room couch. I recall
a tall plastic palm tree in one corner and
down the short hall to one side Dorian's
room, an actor, framed photos of himself
on his walls, some of us joked about that,

his pride mixed with vanity. I recall faces
of people who lived there, also visitors.
When my late friend Bob came to see me
to be with me a few days, back then I took
him into Dinkytown, to Gray's Drugstore
and Valli Pizza. I don't recall moments of

of our being in those places. Only I know they
happened, and though I'll never see him
again, I recall the recent phone calls where
he told me how great it was to see clearly,
how before that operation it was all a blur.
One day I looked out a window and saw him

walking along the side of a house where
as you entered the living room you may
have noticed the fairly tall plastic palm
in the corner. I'm not sure if it was still there
when I moved from that house. I recall you
there, my looking down at your closed eyes.

Lenny Bruce

Something happened, a fucking hard on.
Half asleep, I got up and said to the mirror:
You aren't who I thought you were,
a guy with nothing going on below his belt in his pants.
Whether limp or hard as Chinese arithmetic,
what would America care?
They've got their Cadillacs, their Chevy wagons,
offshore accounts, churches, temples.
In school my teacher said as we get older
physical things matter less and less. I've found,
at forty, they matter more and more.
Americans, the people I know, don't care
about arousal and vibrators. Relationships,
courtships, mortgages, sprinklers and weed killer,
that America is where I live: *Ed Sullivan,
Playhouse 90,* church on Sunday eternal life
through Jesus. Nothing about getting it up,
keeping it up, and don't flaunt, don't go
to a bar alone, and five hundred more don'ts.
But get married, have kids, be a helpmeet.
No one cares about your erogenous self
except Masters and Johnson and clinicians
no one sees because they're tucked away,
away from the churches and malls, the America
of buy and pray, consume and tithe.
Nothing stirring down there, I tell the priest, the rabbi,
the mayor of Pleasantville
where tonight, the two kids in one bed, mom
and dad are watching *Gunsmoke*. A badge flashes,
an outlaw draws a pistol, someone's about to die.

Kids Change Everything

When she was eighteen she gave birth
to a son, Austin, who, his first week,
died a crib death in Arkansas. Austin's
father, while she was pregnant, got shot
and died in her arms. Soon after telling
about Austin she added she got put in jail
for a week over his death. She didn't talk
about him after that and hasn't since.
Then, at forty she gave birth to a girl
who is now five. Kids change everything.
The daughter is real, but I wonder if
there was an Austin who died like that.
Why jail? It's sketchy. I was curious about
her criminal life. Imprisoned two and
a half years, in solitary three times for
fighting. I think she exaggerated and lied.
Did she lie about Austin? Was it really
crib death? Was Austin made up?

Table Talk

L and I at the beach.
She follows me to my parents' house
not close not terribly far from the beach.
An early summer night. My mother
lays out ham, salami, baloney, cheeses
and bread, a light supper.
The table talk is L's car low on gas,
the latch stuck.
Light comes through windows. L
eats a little, worries a lot.
My father gets a device not a crowbar
or anything to damage the tank.
Out front he sizes up, pokes, prods.
My mother and L look over his shoulder.
He pries open the latch finally. L
follows me to the nearest gas station,
then a few miles to a circle where she's
able to get onto a highway that leads
to her parents' home where she's staying.
Not long after this latch incident L
dies in an auto accident, a one-car
fatality. She hits a tree. A few years later
my mother dies in Valley Hospital at the start
of the year, my father at the end at home.
Now they know, L and my parents,
so intent on getting the latch opened.
They know everything, or nothing.

Sideview Mirror

You're thinking about Spencer's *The Faerie Queene*
and how, twenty years ago at a reading
an academic poet, who taught Spencer in university
classes, said Spencer had a lot of trouble
with reality. You're in a Ford dealership
for a new sideview mirror for your 150 pickup. Weather
people on TV report conditions across the country.
It would be easier thinking about Spencer
sipping a diet coke in a fast-food restaurant. Easier
in a city park or while waiting to speak with a loan officer
at a bank. Maybe the people giving the weather,
one or two of them, have read *The Faerie Queene*.
Maybe the academic poet still teaches Spencer.
Maybe *The Faerie Queene* is as fresh and vital to her
today as it was when she herself first read it.
Maybe, since that reading night twenty
years ago, she's found new meaning in it.
Maybe she's read Spencer in Cincinnati
and in Detroit. You yourself must look into it.

White Oval

She sat at the bar, white powder on her face,
red lipstick, eyeshadow, her hair dark,
pulled back tight in a single braid at the back.
She wore a tight black dress. The bar
was shaped like a horseshoe. On the other side
I sat staring, stealing a glance at her.
She'd never looked that vivacious, that alluring.
We'd been lovers. Right from the start
I wanted her to divorce her husband and marry me.
It began in May, abruptly in July she ended it.
We didn't talk anymore, not even hello and goodbye.
Every so often I'd see her in her Augmented
Reality station or in her Camera Array.
That Friday night at the bar, a Venerian cocktail
in front of her, she looked stupendous.
I'd never seen her looking that good. Her face
white, dark hair pulled back in a long braid,
dress tight and black, her eyes and lips colored
to complement her white face. She was all black
and white, astonishingly gorgeous, exotic,
alluring, not saying a word, haunting.

The Unholy Three

The gift wrapped carton of smokes Hector
hands Echo is the irony, a month later Echo/
Lon would die of lung cancer. There he is,
cuffed to a detective, open caboose

platform his stage, hand on brow a salute
to Rosie and Hector, I'll send you a postcard
(from the grave) to them, and to his fans.
The scene before he boards, prison-bound,

between Echo and Rosie, a tear, a smile,
is touching but not as touching as the end
of the silent, done five years before, where
Echo sits on a platform that looks like

a shoeshine stand, in his lap a dummy,
(Echo the ventriloquist in the silent, another
irony.) Indoors, different from the talkie's
train scene. Rosie walks out of the camera's

view. He takes the dummy closer in to his
chest, that subtle embrace, that desire to
hold near, part of Lon's genius. The talkie is
better, but nothing can top the silent's end.

Raymond

My mother's funeral at Our Lady of Refuge
started with a jimmied lock, a break in.

John O' Dwyer shot her, then me, then,
the gun barrel under his chin,
took his own life, twenty-three years ago.
I hovered between life and death.

Today, 1958, Jenna spoons a dollop
of stuffing on her plate and mashes it with a fork.
She's my cousin Ethel's girl.
A begonia suns on a fire escape.
Mint green walls hold our shadows.

My mother's funeral started in a bar
off the Concourse. Glen Miller
on the juke, a man and a woman
slow danced to "At Last."
Another night the man, short, stocky,
sporting a polka dot pocket handkerchief,
leaned and shook my hand.
NYPD but not in uniform, Johnny's
a detective, Mother said.

Seated next to me, my wife, Grace,
blonde, obese. At this Easter table
five children see a tall man with a long
face, a carnation in his lapel.
Grace passes me a bowl of cranberries.
I slice turkey, sip beer from a tall glass.

Downhill a half mile, the Concourse
is quiet. Closed on Sundays,
the shoe outlet that was the Top Club:
Mother stepped from the Ladies.
At the bar O' Dwyer asked,
Can I buy you a drink?

Delicacy

Lloyd, whose surname
will come
when I'm pulling into the bank
or on line at the teller's window,

in an aisle of the cooler
saw me throw a broom
at my boss, Chuck Hinton.
"That was out of character," said

Lloyd of the pressed suit,
the BMW,
a man I could speak to.
Hands folded
at his desk he waited
while I wanted to crawl
the heck out from
under his stare.
Shale Distributing was food.
What Lloyd didn't see
wouldn't hurt him
or Shale, furtively,
down in the freezer. I heated
Cryovac packets of beef
between radiator slats.

Brown bubbles of juice
flavored beef.
I slit open the plastic wrap
and ate the slices.
Warm, delicious going down.

Phone Numbers

I wish I could remember my favorite
afternoon in an art gallery
my favorite night in the mountains
and the most satisfactory moment
I ever had looking at a map.
Today I remembered my parents' last two
phone numbers. I thought how strange
I can no longer telephone and hear
one of their voices, and then the numbers came,
without hesitation: 262-3714 and 262-1228.
That gave me a fleeting satisfaction,
one that didn't last long. Others last
a little longer and a few much longer.
I might have gotten more satisfaction
sitting in a whirlpool at the gym
or sitting back sipping a Scotch on rocks
in a plane at 36,000 feet
than I got this morning in my kitchen,
on a wall the silent telephone.

Summer Night at Heron Lake

Crawdads in a net
gnats in the air mud under your feet
shoe soles and boot soles caked with mud
in the morning after a night of rain
tonight
three mud children a girl two boys
taking crawdads in their hands throwing
the crawdads into a fire
a crawdad covered in ashes crawling
Addy the blonde mud girl
holding one for the first time in her eight
year old hand
Addy standing above the fire
the ground dry the mud gone
from the soles of your boots
Addy with no mother Addy with her father
on a hill above the silver lake
her father in a chair a can of Tecate
in his hand talking with other men women
about sailing
the five month old Zeus
his leash tied to a tree
sniffing the damp ground
the net for crawdads a round meshed
cannister on the ground near the fire pit
the moon half visible through clouds
two kerosene lanterns one on a table one in a tree
the crawdads crawl in ashes
Addy with a thin tree branch moves one into the flames

Two Neighbors

They live across from each other.
The birdbath the blonde Edith
stands next to comes to her waist.
The Edith with dark hair and dark-rim
glasses looks out her window
at the woods: oaks, birches,
pines call to her. The brunette Edith
is closer to the woods, beyond
her backyard a hill of skunk cabbage.
Not one to gab or go out much the brunette
is the inner Edith, her eyes elsewhere.
She is closer to the river. Birds fly
to the smiling, aproned, blonde
Edith's birdbath when she isn't there.

Albert Place

In the face of not knowing what to expect
we're weak though we try to be strong.
Albert Place was shaped like an S.
Dense trees made a dark green dome.
On my bicycle I looked at a yellow
ambulance in front of a small brick house.

Joanne lived there, her father's final hour,
whirling red top of the ambulance.
I pedaled onto that street, turned left
and rode down South Park Drive
onto North Park Drive. On TV Clark Kent
ducked into a washroom, took off
his specs and loosened his tie's Windsor.

Look! Up in the sky! Superman
walked through walls, stopped a maniac
launching a missile, never doubted
a thing, got on with most everyone.
You and me, bending to tie a shoelace
and it breaks, that wasn't him.
In Valley Hospital Joanne stood crying.
Her mother's arm drew her near.

Soldier

1

We give them rifles, metals,
statues to fallen ones.

Who've never been soldiers
don't know what a soldier is.

Who've never been in a war
don't know, just as those

who've never been mothers
or fathers don't know parenthood.

That's natural. It's right
that one war is all wars,

not like but is. War is war.

Soldiers find themselves in a war.
Draftees, volunteers, all said yes.

To the fallen, we place flags
at headstones, erect statues.

The fallen soldiers' metals
sit in a drawer or behind glass

framed and hanging on walls,
the rifles passed on

to soldiers who go to war.

II

Only the soldier knows what a soldier is.
I don't know, though some reading this do,
who are or were. My idea after the soldier
is a civilian he or she stays a soldier.
One could say I was and am no longer.
You, if you've never been, can know what
a soldier is like but not what a soldier is.

They go to war, are in war, fight, whatever
form that takes, part of the war machine
sprawl. All who go choose to go, draftees,
volunteers. Reasons vary: defend a country,
avoid jail, live on the edge, or simply cave
to doing what others want them to do.
Ones who've been in war know what war is.

People living where the war is, they know,
children especially. They have no choice.
Civilians who are part of the war machine
have a choice. In war a few profit.
Many die. War goes against human nature
or maybe it doesn't, two could argue.
If there were no soldiers there'd be no war.

The Door

How exciting it is for some to bring a new
baby home from the hospital. It was for me,
the sibling, the brother. I recall the car ride,
not the hospital, not getting my mother and
the new bundle into the '55 red and black
wagon we had. I vaguely recall the ride.

The door we walked through, red, in time
would be yellow, the door from the screened
porch into the foyer. My father carried his
daughter through that door, a first for him,
for all of us, new life in the house. The door
was big, taking the newborn through it.

She was going from the outside world
into her home, aware, asleep that moment,
in ways a newborn knows, with no word
for door. I recall the sun shining through
a window brightness I felt head to toe. Here
was a new life, blanket wrapped, asleep.

Hillside Stranglers

In Fritz Lang's *M*
filmed in Germany in 1931
Peter Lorre plays the child murderer.
One by one, children disappear
off the streets. Who is it, taking
these lives? Finally found out,
chased, trapped in this huge cellar,
cornered, he turns on the crowd,
wild eyed, flailing, and accuses them.
You murdered the children!
It's in German, so I had only
subtitles, but Lorre, trapped, cornered,
raging, is really good at playing evil.
A versatile, talented actor, he
emigrated from Germany, settled
in Hollywood and played many roles.
His one child, Cathy, in 1977
met up with the Hillside Stranglers,
cousins, Kenneth Bianchi and
Angelo Buono, imprisoned for life
after being convicted of killing numerous
women. They intended to kidnap
and kill her but when they learned she
was Lorre's daughter, so enamored
were these two monsters of Lorre's films,
if anyone deserved to be called
monsters, these two . . . they let her go.

Eighteen

I'd like to say it was Smalls, a landmark,
but it wasn't, it was the Top Club,
almost right across from the Baby Grande,
which in '66 was famous, so I heard.
Scotch and milk, the big drink, the boogaloo
the dance. You extended your arms, waved
them up and down, snapped your fingers
like you were ready to welcome someone
into you, only it wasn't a hugging dance.

John and James had dark skin, John,
a shade darker was called Chip. Times,
if not for Chip I'd have been drinking alone
at the bar. He taught junior high math.
He jabbered, talked quietly and a lot, some
nights to himself. A lot shorter than James,
the big difference, I didn't think of then,
was Chip was alone. James' wife Gloria,
tall with red hair and almond cat's eyes

shook a canister and poured whiskey sours
behind the bar. James was there because
Gloria was, tall and handsome, light skinned
like Velma, who also was a barmaid. Velma,
from Mobile, could sing, but didn't there.
Chip was there, jabbering. Sometimes,
were he not, I'd have been drinking alone.
Though people talked with me: Sonny,
who's surname I've forgotten, Leon Wilson,

a stud in his black lid, cashmere
blond topcoat, pencil mustache, 24,
whereas Sonny, who wore a black leather,
a lid tilted back, a scraggy goatee, was 26.
Velma was 28. She dated Chuck Jackson
once or twice, she said, The Chuck Jackson
of "Any Day Now." He was big. I saw him
at the Apollo, down from the Baby Grande.
Gloria Prince, a barmaid, short, chubby,

looked like the singer Gloria Lynne. Frankie
Smith, like Sonny, wore a black leather
cut past the waist. He never wore a lid.
I visited his room, narrow like a closet. I rode
in James' sedan, with James and Gloria,
their surname Jones, at night on the FDR
above the East River. It was when Viet Nam
was just starting. It wasn't Smalls, a fancier
club, nine blocks up from where we were.

Silent Film Actor

I wrestle a chewed bone from a Rottweiler's jaws
I sing in a choir in St. Patrick's Cathedral
I hold a silent film actor's hand in a cemetery
near a zoo. Don't stop loving me.

I haven't harmed the dog or sung off key or stolen
a bouquet at the foot of a headstone.
I plan to get the actor to his scheduled train
and make certain his niece, Heidi, will be
at his point of arrival.
Maybe on the way to the station we'll stop
in a bar, where I'll buy him a Manhattan
and myself a gin and tonic,

though nothing's certain. I'm not going to
put him on the wrong train or lead him
on foot across a frozen lake.

We're visiting the stones of actors he once knew.
I, who have wrestled a bone from a Rottweiler's jaws
and sung in a church choir, met the actor years ago
in a drugstore in Calais, Maine.

His wife was blonde and beautiful, who now is
ashes. His name is Robert Metzler, whose
niece will meet him at his destination, Washington D.C.
I've never met her. My name is Darrell Moore.
I once lifted a child onto an elephant.
A man, a stranger, led her round the elephant's ring
and nearby was a carousel. That was before I
knew Robert Metzler, before I started singing, before
I came to these stones and found you among the living.

Oh Rosemarie

They were buried in separate cemeteries.

Rosemarie Uva, age 31, and her 29 year old
husband Thomas Uva were in their Mercury
Topaz, in heavy traffic and stopped
at a light when each took three bullets.
The Topaz kept rolling and hit a parked car.
Christmas Eve morning. The Uvas were out
last-minute shopping. Ex-cons, for six
months they'd robbed social clubs allegedly
owned by the Mafia. Christmas Eve
in Ozone Park, her police officer brother
had to tell his mother her daughter's dead.

She had dark brown eyes, long brown hair.

A clear night in December, at the wheel
of the idling Topaz she watched two kids
wearing hoods cross the street.
A jet's roar faded as the plane climbed.
The radio playing "sittin on the dock . . ."
Thomas bolted out the Paradise Club's door.
His Uzi and a bag filled with cash
and jewelry in back, he got in beside her.
They sped off. Three blocks later, riding
shotgun in a Caddy, James Rocco wrote
on a matchbook the Topaz's plate number.

Obscene

A family moves out of a house,
leaves a dog there to starve.

A man says something to a child to make
her feel she is no more
than a chewed piece of gum spit out
in a supermarket parking lot.

Two men in a ring, one kicks the other
in the face.
Two women in a ring: one
breaks the other's kneecap.

The big game hunter gloats
beside the elephant he has shot.

A man lusts for money, for land, for more
than he or his children will ever need.
A woman chases a delusion dreamt up
by a charlatan.

Someone else says: sex is good,
it could be better. When I try to make
the most of it, I'm being obscene.

His Agenda

to place a lens before a leaf in the sun
and evoke a flame
to see a magnificent cottonwood green
in the pale high desert
to see a hawk on a wooden post
to walk at night a runway
where in daylight planes land
to gather mesquite and lay it near a fire pit
to strip naked on a canyon rim and swim in the creek
towel himself dry and put on clean clothes
to put ice and whiskey in a glass
to sit in a chair and open a paperback, Agee's
Let Us Now Praise Famous Men
to fly in a piper cub over a canyon
to see the green cottonwood alone
in a corner of pale high desert
to know the cactus wren is cousin to the javelina
and the sun's dying fire and wind
and egrets white on the Pecos
below fire-blackened trees

Ozu

Yasujiro Ozu's the one for me.
When I was a tyke it was Mickey Mantle,
though my hand eye coordination sucks
and at the plate I couldn't get even a single.
Also Elvis. Age 10 in the mirror I combed my
hair in an Elvis pompadour. JFK, after bald
Ike, was refreshing. Meanwhile in Tokyo

Ozu was making his films, none I knew
till one afternoon in a Hastings aisle, by then
into my fifties, I picked up a DVD I kept.
The black and white photo on its box held
for me a sensuous allure. Suddenly I was
standing in the middle of my living room,
tears streaming down my cheeks,

stunned by *Late Spring,* it turned out to be
my favorite Ozu. You get toward the end.
Setsuko Hara bound, draped, hair
plated and piled, face heavily powdered.
Before Chishu Ryu she prostrates herself.
"Thank you, father, for taking care of me
all these years" is how her words translate.

In a documentary Haruko Sugimura talked
about her circling the room after Noriko
(played by Hara) and her father had gone.
Why she did that, it was instinct, her last
go round the otherwise empty room. How
lesser *Late Spring* had it not been there.
Great seeing her talk about it. Ozu, people

who worked for him called him the master,
camera people, actors. He was the master.
Scenes from many Ozu films in *Tokyo-Ga,*
a Wim Wenders documentary. It shows
a big stone with water spilling down, Ozu's
grave in Tokyo. Some pilgrim there, to Ozu
in that garden, the water sluiced stone.

Speed Reader

Here's a nonfiction tip: Hampton Sides'
In the Kingdom of Ice, a riveting account
of Arctic desolation. Sounds depressing
but the writing redeems it. I found,
when reading, at sea, a Caribbean cruise,
if a fellow passenger had come up,
while I sat in comfort, near a window
that looked out at water and a light sky,
he or she would've had to wrench it
from my hands, so enthralled was I in
Sides' true story of an Arctic venture
at the dawn of the twentieth century.

It was the centerpiece of my cruise,
a book I read quickly, though with most
that's not the case. I read slowly. But
I recall an afternoon in 1971, a ride
from southern Minnesota to South Dakota,
a man, on our return tip, in the back
of a car; the driver I don't recall, nor
the airport where we met this man
who was to lecture at our small and
now defunct college. I recall the man's
wire rim glasses, longish light brown hair,
the brown velour collar of his topcoat.

His clean-shaven face, wide, angular,
chiseled. Some talk prompted him
to say he was a speed reader. I sat
"riding shotgun" in a sedan heading back
to Minnesota, a trip I recall little of, only
little curls came down past his ears.
Speed reader, he said, no boast, his tone
buoyant, matter of fact. I thought what
would that be like, to read a whole page
in ten seconds. Katie, you too may be
a speed reader, but eschew the label.
In the Kingdom of Ice is a real good read.

A Man Like a Tree

"Sparky almost checked out
of the hotel of life,"
is what you say when a man
past eighty falls from
a small scaffold his
California daughter told him
recently to get rid of.
If years could be measured
in height, Sparky'd be
a sequoia — though he
didn't say that, but did
speak of the fall,
the bruised arm, aching shoulder
and said this in what
had been the Commercial
Hotel, founded by his dad,
whose picture, a color
daguerreotype, hangs
above the lobby desk
looking handsome, sapling young.

Leave

There's the door, the night.
Go out into it. Leave.

Down from my apartment
in a park a Sunday concert,
a heart surgeon said of home,
"I don't miss it."

Leave,
like the leaves on trees.
Faces we'll never see again,
an ocean lies between us.

But there's the Chapel of Hope.
I enter. In the casket lies Roy,
my eldest friend.

Gone but not like the fugitive
hops a boxcar,
or the detective's sidekick
turns through the revolving wall.

Only death is certain.
Roy in the locker room laced his shoes,
getting ready to walk upstairs,
out the gym door to his parked Cadillac.

Sleeping with a Student

I

The book is open.
Leaves on the trees are dull green.
We muddle through: no absolutes,
no one answer, no one person says
I'm the one with the answers.
We muddle through the book,
through the traffic of sidewalk pedestrians.
No step-by-step guide,
no full dark beard to disguise who I am.
No, but sometimes I wear a mask
so I don't even recognize myself.
We muddle through: our hands
in tool chests search for the right wrench.
We muddle through wind and rain,
the paper mill stench
one night in late September
riding with a man who learned
English from the writer John Kennedy Toole
and piano from Toole's mother.

II

We muddle through the tunnel named
after Lincoln and the tunnel unnamed
and muddle through a parking lot
listening to Lee Dorsey or Johnnie Taylor's
song about celebrities in heaven.
We muddle through light
and through pages of a paperback
Confederacy of Dunces. Muddle
through a pet shop, wall to wall
cages. Muddle through a spacious
dining room with doors
leading out to gardens of purple,
white and blue flowers. Muddle
through directories and classifieds
and cupboards needing canned goods,
cupboards like minds waiting to be filled.
To muddle through means man,
horse and tree live together.
The man with the book wears a full dark beard.

III

The face of the man I rode with
that night near the paper mill,
the man who knew the author before
he was an author, before he was dead —
I remember his driving, his voice,
his face growing vaguer each year.
I knew the ex-wife of the man
who sat with his students under a tree
and with an open book in his hand
said, "We muddle through."
I also knew the student he was sleeping with.
She was with him that next winter
when he had a heart attack.
He wore a full dark beard.
When he said we muddle through
he was responding to words
in the book they'd been discussing,
he and his students,
among them Sandra, his lover.

IV

We muddle through dull days,
sleepless nights, visits from uninvited guests,
expected and unexpected phone calls.
Muddle through the produce aisle
and the marina. Muddle through the texts
and the silence in cages where animals sleep.
Muddle through divorce, hospital,
committee meeting. Good luck,
I say to Charlene, the bearded man's
ex-wife. She's getting up from the table
to leave. Muddle through: no one
truth but many. No black and white
but gray. The perplexity, the many sides,
the pondering. The guess, the mistake,
the fall, the daylight, the chance —
all talked about under the tree.

Capitalists

Nancy Sidley owns the delegation. Pale,
seated in rows of straight-back chairs
they look like mirrors in storage.
She knows the violins will be played
not smashed over wrestlers' heads
in a ring at the armory.

She knows the ups and downs of fear,
the dead eyes of outlaws she's seen
while brushing her hair in a mirror.
Evelyn owns a compost, Adele and Adolph
a tall oak at the bottom of a hill.
Walking in that oak's shade Nancy

has heard and felt acorns crunch.
Bill owns the champagne magnums,
and the suave look he wears
at the Labor Day carnival. Someone
owns the Ferris wheel. Nancy
doesn't know who, but she knows Frank

owns lumber, Jack a pair of dice,
Dennis and Regina the Manor Tavern
and Margaret a pearl handled switchblade
found one Saturday morning in the street
after she stepped out her door.
She put it in her jeans back pocket

and kept walking. At the Candy Store
of Eternity, owned by Otto, she made sure
no one saw the knife. At home,
in her room with the door shut, Margaret,
seeing her reflection in a mirror,
pushed a button, up sprang the blade.

Richard Pryor

I sat way up in the balcony.
In the spotlight on stage,
a slim twenty something:
confident in his hands,
his eyes roving the orchestra,
the tiered balcony,
Richard Pryor cracking jokes rapid fire:
mimicry, insane laughter
rising like a wave, carrying us,
he was there, the one, the me-ness
of pay-attention, effortless,
vivid. The short Afro, thin tie,
hands going to the tie knot. Then,
spin the time dial ahead
forty years: his darkness,
his wheelchair, head tilted
sideways, eyes staring
where no one else was looking,
a wheelchair's blanket over
his legs. Are you cold?

Negative

Negative, negative, negative,
Don said to Scotty.
Now, nothing to be negative about
for these teachers of math,
Don retired in Utah,
Scotty a name on a stone,
a cemetery dweller
whose home was once a math class,
and a pie-shaped house
that he himself designed.
No negatives side by side with positives,
coming to terms, or not, in some hereafter.
Scotty with his lurching walk,
hospital visits to students
to give them homework.
And Don, once a patient tended by nurses
that were students in his classes.
Don in Utah, Scotty nowhere,
that zero of all zeros, thinner than air,
finer than dust, that house
we see by faith only, or don't see,
no faith in God; or, in a God
who, withholding a hereafter, is negative.

I recall Don's rimless glasses, his knack
for compromise,
and Scotty's gun cabinet,
the fishing rod in his hand at the San Juan
River.
His shadowy voice, sort of deep and
angular,
the Camels smoked occasionally,
the swear words spoken often.
A gay irreverence, not surly
but at times a negative outlook, except,
I suppose, when it came to math.
Some said he was a genius,
could have taught anywhere.
I recall the brace on his knee
from an old basketball injury,
and his last words, my last look
as he shut my pickup's door
and walked towards his house
which I'd been in, many times.
I recall standing beside him on the Rio
Grande's banks,
that river that flows between two countries.

Sweating in the Freezer

Trying to write a poem
of how bitter the winter cold was today on the dock.
It was warmer in the freezer.
I had to duck inside the freezer to be warm.
On the dock it was so cold.
Ordinarily I never have to work,
but this morning I had to go out to take the mini maple
hams and the Hillshire frozen sausages off the trail end
of the truck.
I was riding on the forklift.
The dark blue forklift against silver winter sky,
the backdrop of ugly steel structures.
What an ugly part of town this is!

But you're so damn cold
that who has time to notice it.
This ache in my knee
that wants to play
on your sympathy
as I write here tonight
hearing dreadful music
my legs crossed
sitting on the sofa
notices it is
thinking about the dock.

The word was out that the inspector
was approaching the shipping department,
we had to take all the corn beef rounds,
pumped with water
for bigger profits,

and hide them down in the south freezer.
It was warmer in the freezer
than out on the dock. I toppled
a pallet of corn beef rounds.
Rex came down to help me
pick them up and said it was
immoral to handle this stuff,
everyone who buys it
will be getting screwed.
He was right,
but it was so cold
going in and out
from the freezer
to the dock.
It's the coldest place in the world
when the wind whips along the dock.

Does anyone know what it feels like when
the external parts of the body
begin to get warm
leaving the residue,
an internal chill?

Double Elegy

An outdoor bar shaded by palm trees,
your husband's arm around your shoulder.
On the bar, two margaritas. You smile
in this picture taken four years ago.

It's displayed with others up on the screen,
pictures of you from your teens
till the present. Their lights and shadows
differ from the light and dark
at midday in the chapel. You're up front,
laid out, except it doesn't look like you.

At Johnson-Miller, I'd sit across your desk
from you. Take a vacation, I would say.
I'd sit across your desk from you
and you'd make me laugh so hard I'd cry.

*

Years ago I kissed a girl at a drive in movie.
Later she became a woman.
Then a woman dying in a hospice.
Her ashes were scattered off the Florida coast.

On her deathbed she asked a friend,
Is there something after this?

Third Wheel

Alan and Jeanne were walking,
as was I,
with big trees all around and the sky
more dark than light.

Their apartment
was on the ground floor. We had coffee.
I put on my coat and walked the quarter
mile to my house.

It was before I had a car.
It was late winter.
We were together no more than an hour.
Alan and Jeanne had light brown hair,

only Jeanne's was down her back,
Alan's thin on top. His beard was dark.
They were from England, but met here
in the States.

He taught at the university,
she was in nursing school.
He'd published three novels.
Both he and Jeanne were quiet,

friendly, not inclined to boast.
She was quietly pretty, medium height,
slender but not thin.
If I had that hour back

I'd suggest we meet for dinner
at a place close enough to walk to.
They could walk in and see me,
or I them, if they got there first.

Then I Remembered

But can't, if I drove her to the party,
I may have, I think so but maybe not.
Maybe she drove and met me. Maybe
we stood together in the dark and I
rang a doorbell. K's kitchen counter
strewn with bottles, K loomed large like
his male cousin, and his cousin's wife.
They'd driven from Oklahoma, she was
an indigenous person, their names I
can't recall. Jimmy was there, loud and
wasted. I myself, when I walked out,
got in my pickup, was too drunk to drive.
Next day she told me, maybe by phone
maybe face to face how K and his cousin
pawed her. I picture K's big hand on
her shoulder, K's hand wants to go down
to her left breast. She's had a lot to drink
but she steps away; then the cousin paws
her thigh, she's in a tight black dress, they
were half wasted, they wanted her down
on the couch, or maybe the kitchen floor.
All she told me was . . . I don't remember
if she said rape, she may have. I won't
ask her, we live far apart, and why bring
it up, she might want me to.

Small Daughter

I don't remember begging my father
for a leather whip, but he bought my brother
and me leather whips in upstate New York
the summer we went to a tent show run by
a man who more than likely cracked a whip.
I don't remember: gee, I want one like his,

or an assistant, or whip tricks
like an assistant holds in her hand a paper
dove a lash shatters, or the man fires
blanks from a pistol at a grinning paper bear
target, but he wore fringed buckskin
and in the tent starred in a Wild West show.

He'd starred in a TV western until cancer
of the larynx forced him off TV. Here he was,
a tent master in the summer night. He rode
a horse around a ring, an audience clapped.
I mostly remember the show ended, he
told his small daughter if she couldn't keep

her dog quiet he'd take it out and shoot it.
Somehow I knew she was his daughter,
a pup in her arms as he spoke sharply.
I knew also he starred in a TV commercial:
he swam to a dock in a lake, as he sat
on the dock a young woman draped a towel

on his shoulders, and gave him a bottle of
Coke, before his voice changed so it was
no good for TV. I don't remember the show
he'd starred in, only his tent show, everyone
getting up to leave, him towards the back
scolding her so it wouldn't happen again.

Revise

How great to go back: still, the forked
branch, the string, the rubber bands,
the chamois like leather a pouch
for the stone. I grip the fork's stick,
draw the sling, the stone hits a rabbit
that sprints into a copse of trees,
grazed only, intact to keep on doing
what rabbits do. To you a long life,
Rabbit. My new target a sparrow in flight
my stone doesn't touch. Still no good
with the slingshot he made for me.
Now is not then. I show it to George Roth
who lives across the street, to Paul Caples
and Fred Reed. Can I try it out? asks Paul.
His stone pings off a tarnished tin garbage
can at a curb. This go round I don't get
frustrated. Up in my room the slingshot
doesn't lie broken on a rug that covers
speckled linoleum, broken like a jay,
its wings stilled by a boy's stone.
This time I tell him what he made for me
I take into woods. I hit elm trunks;
that will do. I like the draw of the sling.
The stone's release stops no rabbit's
heart deep in the woods.

Ink Factory

Hanson at the ink factory all day on a line
looking at bottles of blue ink, black
and red ink, thought of a toilet bowl factory,

a doorknob factory, a sign factory,
signs such as "Get this over quick"
and "It never gets any better than this."

He thought of a factory of wire elephants
and giraffes, and factories with everything
taken out: shelves, pallets, hydraulic lifts.

Emptiness factories: here's emptiness:
empty boxes, empty shelves.
The wire elephants and giraffes have risen,

have been packed and sent to Siberia.
He thought of his sister-in-law Ethel
getting acquainted with Nancy at a bar,

"I make paste and put the paste in jars.
Kids in schools cut out trees, clouds,
picket fences they paste on paper.

The good cut outs get tacked
to walls." He thought of a tack factory
and a factory for industrial slings.

James and Miss Q

I was seven, a second grade failure.
James Wilson and Miss Q
were rolling around on the floor.
Fast, quiet, a turbulent, human brew.

James, in the back, gets up from his desk,
his head a glazed melon, hair like weeds,
puffed cheeks, puffy eyes like slits.
He pulls from his dungarees

back pocket a grimy, folded paper
he doesn't open, crude
penciled numbers or alphabet letters.
All I know, it's his homework. Miss Q,

up front, says, Give me that mess.
In her blond perm, hourglass shape born
for a business suit she means business.
It happens quickly, their storm.

Light through windows falls on zigzag desk
rows. They roll on the floor in the room,
scuffle, over smudged asterisks
or Bs and Cs he'd struggled to form.

Acknowledgements

The author thanks the following journals in which these poems originally appeared:

Divot, Flights of the Dragonfly, Dead Peasant, BlazeVOX, Bluepepper, Ephemeral Elegies, Erothanatos, Electric Rail, Exterminating Angel, Founders Favourites, Nauseated Drive, 411, Bardball, Mad Swirl, The Antonym, Misery Tourism, Cacti Fur, Punk Noir, Cerasus, Open Door, Punk Monk, The Five Two, Art Villa, Yellow Mama, Home Planet News, Red Wolf Journal, The Big Windows Review, As above So Below, Indiana Literary Journal, BOMBFIRE, Boomer Lit Mag, Capella, The City Key, Quail Belle, Bez & Co, The Pangolin Review, Piker Press, Granfalloon, Alternate Route, Raw Dog Press, The Stickman Review, Milk Carton Blog, Poetic Sun, Circumference, Rye Whiskey Review, Brazos River Review, New Note Poetry, Our Day's Encounter, Poetry Super Highway, Adelaide Literary Review, October Hill, The Westbere Review, Roi Faineant Press, and *Moss Piglet*.

About the Author

Peter Mladinic lives in Hobbs, New Mexico. He was born and raised in New Jersey and has lived in the Midwest and in the South. He enlisted in the United States Navy and served for four years. He received an MFA in Creative Writing from the University of Arkansas in 1985, and taught English for thirty years at New Mexico Junior College in Hobbs. He has edited two books: *Love, Death, and the Plains*, and *Ethnic Lea: Southeast New Mexico Stories,* which are available from the Lea County Museum Press, as are three volumes of poetry: *Lost in Lea, Dressed for Winter,* and *Falling Awake in Lovington.* His most recent book, *Knives on a Table* was published by Better Than Starbucks Publications in 2021. He is a past board member of the Lea County Museum and a former president of the Lea County Humane Society. An animal advocate, he supports numerous animal rescue groups. Two of his main concerns are to bring an end to the euthanizing of animals in shelters and to help get those animals adopted into caring homes.

www.ingramcontent.com/pod-product-compliance
Lightning Source LLC
Chambersburg PA
CBHW071354080526
44587CB00017B/3095